CHURCH, STATE, MORALITY AND LAW

Patrick Hannon

D0544390

Gill and Macmillan

Published in Ireland by
Gill and Macmillan Ltd
Goldenbridge
Dublin 8
with associated companies in
Auckland, Budapest, Gaborone, Harare, Hong Kong,
Kampala, Kuala Lumpur, Lagos, London, Madras,
Manzini, Melbourne, Mexico City, Nairobi,
New York, Singapore, Sydney, Tokyo, Windhoek
© Patrick Hannon 1992
0 7171 1978 5
Print origination by
Seton Music Graphics Ltd, Bantry, Co. Cork
Printed by
Colour Books Ltd, Dublin

A catalogue record is available for this book from the British Library.

In Gratitude to my Parents

Contents

FOREWORD

This book is concerned with the question, how is a Catholic expected to vote on certain types of issue involving morality and law? The question has arisen at regular intervals in recent Irish experience but it is not confined to Ireland; and in particular, unexpectedly perhaps, it is a subject of continuing discussion in the United States since the presidential election campaign of 1984. The book's objective is to sketch an approach from within Catholic theology which would offer the possibility of a coherent and consistent framework of response.

That the question should arise at all requires some explanation, and an explanation is offered in the opening chapter. Every society has to face the problem of the embodiment of its values in its laws. And where there are diverse moral value systems the question is inevitable: whose values, or which, are to be reflected in legislation? When a particular moral belief is associated with the teaching of a particular Church it is easy to think that the debate is about the embodiment of that Church's values in the law of the land.

Law-making always involves a balancing of individual freedom with the requirements of life in society. It cannot be expected to give a right to do harm or to allow the exercise of the rights of one at the expense of the rights of others. It seeks to harmonise the exercise of freedoms so that each person may have prospect of flourishing to the best of his or her own potential. It is therefore concerned with peace in the community, with preventing or ending destructive conflict and with promoting harmonious relationships. It is concerned also with justice, with securing and defending people's rights and with offering the chance of redress. And it cannot but be concerned with other moral values too, with ways of being and behaving which people think of as right or wrong, good or bad, inasmuch as they enhance or diminish the flourishing of a human being.

But here a problem may arise, for people differ as to what makes for human flourishing. This should not be exaggerated; there are many things which are almost self-evidently enhancing or diminishing of humanity. Few would doubt that life should be protected or that fidelity is good, or that one ought not to cheat or tell lies. But not everyone believes that artificial contraception is wrong, or that it is always wrong to re-marry while a spouse is still alive, or that it is never right deliberately to end a pregnancy. And so a question arises, whose morality, what law?

And of course even when people agree as to what is morally right or wrong, they may differ about how the law should reflect their beliefs. It is possible to abhor pornography and yet to think that legal censorship is not the way to deal with it. One might believe that homosexual activity is wrong and yet oppose its prohibition by the criminal law. It is easy to see that adultery is incompatible with a belief in the value of fidelity in marriage but it does not follow that it should be punished by the law of the land.

Questions about the relationship between morality and the law are not confined to issues of sexual morality and associated realms. Laws which aim to end discrimination against women or on the basis of colour or race are no less of moral concern. Nor is the question of the enforcement of morals the only one which may arise regarding the relationships between morality and law. But it is a recurrently practical one, especially in reference to sexual *mores*; and in the way in which it arises for Catholics it is focal for many concerns of the Catholic Church's self-understanding in the present day.

It is a central contention of this book that the question for Catholics is at its core the same as for any politician or citizen. Why then make ado about what is 'expected' of Catholics in particular? One obvious reason is that in the Roman Catholic Church there is a strong tradition of the authoritative exercise of a teaching function. And this *magisterium* is perceived, outside as well as inside that Church, as making a claim on the consciences of members. When bishops make their mind known upon a proposal to make or change a law people wonder whether or to what extent Catholics are expected to obey them.

Our question then is complex, and in order to achieve a clear view of it we must attend to diverse themes. Considered in its broadest terms it concerns the interrelationships and interactions between morality, religion and the law. Religion and morality are intimately related in the experience of many societies, so much so that it is uncommonly difficult to hold the distinction between them relevantly in view. Similarly for morality and law; the mere fact that in some ways they *look* alike can make it difficult to grasp that they are not at all the same thing. Chapter 2 sketches some salient features of each, with special attention to the ways in which they bear upon each other in terms of our concerns.

The standpoint of the book is that of contemporary Catholic theology, but all christian theologising must try to keep faith with the Scripture. Two things in particular interest us: how the New Testament understands morality, and what the young Church made of its relationship to the civil society. These are the concerns of chapter 3.

The present self-understanding of the Catholic Church is a more immediate backdrop to our question, and chapter 4 selects from the skeins of which it is woven some which contribute to the question's sharper definition. First some pertinent themes of the Second Vatican Council are recalled: the relationship between Church and world, the 'autonomy' of secular matters, the particular competence of lay members, the significance of hierarchical ministry. These themes inform and shape our conception of Church today; and the concept of Church to which they lead is explored with the aid of an analysis made by Avery Dulles.

In the Roman Catholic theology of Church a theme of obvious importance is that of *magisterium*, the teaching role and competence of the hierarchy. At least some of the confusion which people experience concerning the intervention of church leadership in public debate stems from confusion about the character and scope of *magisterium*. Does theology require one to take a bishops' Conference as the voice of God, or are bishops just another interest-group in the community—or *how* are their interventions to be understood? Chapter 5 examines the nature and function of teaching authority in the Church, especially in its bearing upon concrete moral direction; and chapter 6 offers some reflections on the exercise of teaching by bishops' Conferences.

Chapter 7 brings us to the centre of the enterprise, for it proposes a framework within which the focal question may be viewed. The contention is, in short, that the *Declaration on Religious Freedom* of the Second Vatican Council furnishes a framework and the basic principles for coping with all particular questions concerning the enforcement of morality by the law. The Council's teaching was about religious (as distinct from moral) freedom, and its application to morality must be argued for. I shall argue that it may in fact be so applied; and that in moral as in religious matters people should not be made to act against their consciences nor restrained from acting according to conscience—subject to the requirements of the common good.

Clearly this proviso is of the greatest significance, and its import is explored in chapters 8 and 9. In Catholic usage the expression 'common good' refers to the ensemble of conditions of social living which make for the fullest possible flourishing of each member of the community.

According to a standard enumeration of its components it includes a
'public morality', which qualifies the freedom of individual members, and
which it may be the business of the law to enforce. What *this* means has
been the subject of a famous debate between Sir Patrick (now Lord)
Devlin and Professor H.L.A. Hart and their many commentators. The
protagonists stand for positions which may respectively be called conservative and liberal. What each has to say is valuable in helping us make
sense of our own reactions. An important aspect of my own submission is
that neither is particularly 'the Catholic view'.

Chapter 10 supposes that the argument will have left some readers
uneasy. Two types of reader are envisaged, one a believer, the other a
critic, each sceptical of the freedom for which the book contends. By
way of an exploration of some of the requirements of an effective
presence of the Church in today's world an attempt is made to show
that neither need be suspicious.

It is now a kind of fashion for authors to direct readers to what they
conceive to be the main or most important parts of the book. One
wonders whether this isn't an admission that the rest is padding, an
implication which any writer would doubtless wish to resist. Yet there
is something to be said here for the suggestion that after reading the
first two chapters the reader might go to chapter 7, where the heart of
the argument is to be found. Chapters 8 and 9 follow naturally and
necessarily; and chapter 10 rounds off the argument. I hope, though,
that a reader who takes this path might in the end be tempted to return
to chapters 3 to 6. For these chapters disclose a broader canvas and they
intimate our subject's depth, and the theological understandings to
which they point inform the treatment as a whole.

Another authorial fashion, this time age-old, is to proclaim the
modesty of the undertaking and to insist that there is more to be said
on the subject-matter than has been possible in the present work.
A glance through this book will show that such a disclaimer is more
than usually superfluous. Again and again, topics of great intrinsic
importance are barely opened up, and the main subject-matter is at best
a contribution to and certainly not the end of discussion. The objective
has been to lay out the principles which should ground an approach to
specific issues in the realm of the book's concern, and to offer some
suggestions concerning their practical application. The hope is that a
reader will thereby be helped to reach his or her own conclusions.

I hope that this book may be of use not just to the professional
student of theology but to anyone interested in the themes with which

it deals. That indeed is one of the reasons why it incorporates an introduction to the theology of morals as understood in Roman Catholicism, and that it opens up some major themes in Catholic theology since the Second Vatican Council. In the same spirit, references are on the whole confined to standard material readily available in English; and *that* material may prompt the reader onwards.

Finally, a word about two choices the effect of which will irritate some. I use the expression 'Roman Catholic' often enough, I hope, to indicate an awareness of the importance of the qualifier in an ecumenical perspective. But, however regrettably, it is not a colloquial usage in Ireland, and I have felt it more natural to omit, in most cases, the 'Roman'. I hope that no-one is offended. The second choice was not to amend the sexist language of material quoted from other sources; copyright questions are only the most obvious obstacle.

1

Church, State, Morality
and Law

From time to time during the past two decades Ireland has witnessed a public debate concerning the enforcement of morality by law. The arena of the debate has mainly been the Republic, though there has also been discussion about the law of Northern Ireland; and the southern debate has been seen by some as having an important northern reference. The topics debated have by and large been in the domain of sexual and family morality: in the Republic, contraception, abortion, divorce and homosexual practices; in the north the two last mentioned.

At one level these debates have been about the embodiment of moral beliefs in the law. Divorce, for example, is for most people a moral issue: that is, most people have a view as to whether or not it is forbidden by the moral law. But in the Republic of Ireland it is forbidden also by the law of the land, for the Irish Constitution prohibits the enactment of legislation which would make divorce available. The desirability of changing the Constitution in this respect is debated from time to time, and on the face of it the debate is about the relationship between a moral belief and the law of the state.

But such debates are also often seen as having to do with the relationship between Church and State. And the reason for this is plain: morality is taken to be the province of the 'Church', the law the business of the 'State'. In the divorce debate the moral belief in question—usually referred to as the indissolubility of marriage—is associated especially with the Christian religion. It is therefore easy to envisage the issue as one of expressing in the secular law a Christian moral belief.

The matter is complicated by the fact that there are differences of interpretation of the principle of indissolubility as between the Christian Churches themselves. A 'strong' version of the principle is associated with the Roman Catholic tradition, and Roman Catholicism is the religion of the majority in the Republic. It is easy to see how the debate might in these circumstances be thought to be about the embodiment of Catholic doctrine in the Constitution. And here another factor enters in. Churches are often identified in the public mind with their leaderships, and church doctrines are thought to be the province of the leaders especially. This is perhaps particularly so in the case of the Catholic Church, the leadership of which characteristically displays what in current jargon is called a high profile. Similarly the State is often identified with its institutions, and especially with government and laws. In the most recent divorce debate in Ireland the leadership of the Catholic Church opposed a government proposal to amend the Constitution, while the leaders of other Churches did not. It is not surprising that the debate was seen as involving the relationship of the Catholic Church to the State.

There is yet another way of viewing such a debate, and that is as a matter of the rights of minorities in a pluralist society. In Ireland, minority in this context refers of course to the membership of Churches other than the Catholic, but it includes people of no religious affiliation; and indeed it may include some Catholics, either because they do not accept the principle of the indissolubility of marriage or—what is probably more usual—because they consider that divorce should be available to those who have no conscientious objection to it. A pluralist society in the context is one in which there is a *de facto* diversity of belief concerning the morality of divorce. The contention is that the law should respect this diversity and should not preclude divorce in the case of people who believe that they are morally entitled to avail themselves of it.

People from other countries, even from the traditionally Roman Catholic, often express surprise that matters such as these are still debated in Ireland, for it is taken to be a mark of liberal democracy that allowance is made by its institutions for religious and moral pluralism. Indeed Ireland's tardiness in accommodating to pluralism is sometimes regarded as evidence of an insular backwardness, a condition usually attributed at least in part to a paralysing dominance of the Roman Catholic clerisy. This unflattering appraisal of the Irish spirit seems indifferent to the fact that the issues of principle which underlie the debates are capable of perplexing people of quite other religious and moral and cultural inheritance.

The United States, to take an instructive example, is also witnessing a new debate upon the principles involved. The example is instructive in that, pluralist in its very foundations, that country from the beginning has had to reckon with questions which came only later to many European countries. It might have been thought that its entire experience, shaped by a constitutional principle providing alike for the separation of Church and State and for the free exercise of religion, must by now have resolved any problems of theory or of practice involved in the work of legislation in a situation of religious and moral pluralism. Yet for most of the past decade a debate has raged in which all of the principles which have shaped the US experience have been brought under fresh scrutiny.

That debate is about the law on abortion. Again the problem is that of the expression of a moral belief through the medium of law. In the slogans familiar from US discussion, some believe that a woman has a *right to choose* to abort an unwanted pregnancy, others in a foetus' prior *right to life*. In 1973 a decision of the Supreme Court interpreted the Constitution of the United States as favouring the former view and—though there are signs just now of second thoughts—that interpretation still prevails. Meanwhile people who uphold the foetus' right to life have been campaigning for a change. And to the fore in this group has been the leadership of the Catholic Church.

Again therefore a question about morality and the law takes on the colour of an issue in the relationship between Church and State; and again it is often canvassed in terms of what is appropriate or not in a pluralist society. These latter dimensions were pointed up sharply in the course of the 1984 presidential election campaign. The Democratic vice-presidential candidate Geraldine Ferraro, asked what she proposed to do about the law on abortion, distinguished between her belief as a Catholic that abortion is wrong and her duty as a politician in a pluralist society to favour a law which would give women a right to choose. Her reply gave rise to a debate which has not yet ended and to which we must later return. For the US debate, even if unfinished, has contributed much to a better understanding of the issues.

The Question

The central question with which this book is concerned is, how is a Catholic legislator or citizen expected to vote when matters of this sort fall to be decided? The word 'expected' is chosen because it can refer to what people, including outside observers, can reasonably anticipate when Catholics come to decide this type of question; but also because it intimates some kind of *obligation,* in virtue of which a Catholic may be required by church leadership or by conscience to vote in one way rather than in another. The aim is to sketch a framework within which someone who wishes to be faithful to a Catholic tradition may look at such issues as they arise.

It might seem that it should suffice to invoke general principles concerning the embodiment of moral beliefs in law, and there is indeed a crucial sense in which that is so. For, as was remarked earlier, the questions at stake are not exclusively Catholic; and I shall later stress that the debates are *essentially* about morality and law, and that when this fact is obscured there is confusion. But in practice these questions are often multi-layered: they often also involve the relationship between Church and State, and they lead to the question of minority rights in a morally pluralist society. A book which aims to deal with morality and law in a Catholic context must advert to these dimensions too.

I have said that at the book's core is the question, how is a Catholic expected to vote when matters of this sort fall to be decided? I have in mind the fact that Catholics are often puzzled as to their responsibilities at such moments—as indeed are others. Is a Catholic obliged to try to have his or her Church's moral beliefs enshrined in the law of the State? After all, anyone who holds strongly to a moral belief must surely wish that it receive the maximum possible recognition in society at large. And when it comes to voting, as legislators or as citizens, are Catholics bound to follow the direction of their church leaders? After all they believe that the pope and the bishops are helped by the Holy Spirit in the task of guiding the Church. What *is* the domain of the Spirit's assistance?

As it happens there is much explicit guidance in the directives offered by leaders. In the divorce debate in Ireland the Catholic bishops made use of an approach which has characterised their Conference's interventions in debates on issues of law and morality since the early seventies. At the core of the approach is both an affirmation of the citizen's freedom to vote as he or she wishes and a statement of the bishops' own objections to change. But what is to be made of this? Are the bishops' objections just another opinion in the discussion, or, as representing the considered position of the Church's leadership, are they somehow binding on the Catholic conscience? What, when it comes to voting, *ought* a Catholic do?

The approach of the bishops relies upon the distinction between a moral belief and the expression of that belief in law, and it acknowledges that the latter is a matter of the political or civic judgment of legislators or voters. That distinction and acknowledgment are not novel; we shall see that they have a distinguished ancestry. More recently they lay behind the response of John F. Kennedy in 1960 to the question whether as a Catholic he was bound to promote the specific beliefs of the Catholic Church in the event of his becoming President of the

United States. And they appear to have been acceptable to the Church leaders of the time.

What then of the reply of Ms Ferraro mentioned above? It—or, more accurately, its articulation by other leading US politicians—was criticised by Archbishop (now Cardinal) John O'Connor of New York, at least partly on the basis that it is wrong to make a sharp distinction between moral beliefs and political stances. On the face of it Ms Ferraro seemed to be saying no more than John Kennedy did. So what is the Catholic politician or voter to think or do?

Objectives

What is most fundamentally needed is a framework in which the issues may be viewed in a fashion which is consistent and coherent. And I shall argue here that the Church's own teaching provides such a framework, and that the framework is to be found in the *Declaration on Religious Freedom* of the Second Vatican Council. At the heart of the argument is the proposition that the stance of Catholicism *vis-à-vis* freedom of moral belief and practice in civil society is analogous to its stance in the sphere of religious belief and practice. The framework thus furnished does not yield neat and instant answers in every concrete case. But it does offer the possibility of an approach which is both consistent and coherent with Church doctrine and tradition, while responsive to modern social reality.

The doctrine of the *Declaration* does not occur in a vacuum, and indeed it has a history which has its own interest, though we shall not have time to go into that. But it also has a context in contemporary theology of the Church—in the more general theology of Vatican Two as this is found in other important documents of the Council—and in subsequent theological reflection. We shall glance too at that context, and at some especially relevant strands in the Catholic Church's understanding of itself today. For a Catholic approach to the question with which we are concerned is ultimately shaped by the way in which the Church understands itself and its mission in the world.

Ten years ago Liam Ryan essayed a statement of the role of the Catholic Church in Irish politics in the future and what he had to say is applicable in western society generally. For Ryan the main question facing the Catholic Church now is not that of relationships between clerical and lay, liberal and conservative, preconciliar traditionalist and postconciliar reformist, or even between Catholic and Protestant; these, he says are internal squabbles which have always been part of organised

religion. 'Rather the problem is: where does the Church stand in relation to the whole structure of modern civilisation? The question for the
Church is how it conceives its relationship, not with the State, but with
society as a whole.'[1]

Ryan's essay was a reflection upon past and present Irish experience
and it took as its starting-point a remark of John Whyte in his
distinguished study of the relationship between the Catholic Church
and the State in Ireland: 'The extent of the hierarchy's influence in Irish
politics is by no means easy to define. The theocratic state model on
the one hand, and the Church-as-just-another-interest-group on the
other, can both be ruled out as oversimplified, but it is by no means
easy to present a satisfactory model intermediate between these two'.[2]
Liam Ryan's thesis was that the role of the Church henceforward is to
act as *conscience* of society.

This idea was taken up by Enda McDonagh who while granting its
merit has formulated certain questions in its regard: 'Is the Church the
only conscience of society? Who as Church shall speak for the conscience
of society? Is this a task for the bishops only, or bishops and priests, or
the laity? Is it an ecumenical task for the Churches working together, or
one for the Catholic Church only? On what issues shall this conscience
be voiced, on the traditional issues of sexual morality, respect for life in
terms of abortion or political violence, on education, or is there a whole
wider range of issues? How are these issues discerned? How are
conscience judgments formed about them? Who shall listen to this
conscience? How shall its judgment be offered or imposed?'[3]

There can be no question here of a treatment of these questions
which would do full justice to their complexity and their range. But
they serve to indicate the breadth of the canvas of our concern, supplying
pointers to the kind of issue to which we shall have to give at least a
modicum of attention. And so the lineaments of a map of our exploration
suggest themselves.

A Map

Our concern is with morality as it is understood in the Catholic
tradition, and we shall need to think about what we mean by this. In
particular we must try to clarify the relationships, or some of them,
between morality and Christian faith and between morality and law, for
a good deal of our confusion is founded upon misconception on these
scores. I shall say that since right moral living is an inescapable demand
of the teaching of Christ, moral witness is an inescapable aspect of the

mission of the Church in the world, and moral teaching a part of the function of Church leadership. But I am going to stress that the Christian message is not to be reduced to a message about right moral living; and that when it is, there results a moralism which is both an impoverishment of the Christian gospel and a stumbling-block for many people of good will.

And that raises the question of the Church's conception of itself today. It is no doubt something of a simplification (though nonetheless true) to say that the Second Vatican Council heralded a movement from an institutional concept to one which emphasises community; from a hierarchical conception to one of a people going forward in pilgrimage to an eschatological destiny; from a model in which authority 'reigned' to one in which the hierarchs are seen as servants. What is incontrovertible is that the Council set the seal on developments in the theory and practice of Church living which are of the utmost importance for the concerns of this book.

One of these developments was ecumenism: on the Catholic side, combined with a belief that the Church of Christ 'subsists in' that Church, a recognition of the value of other traditions, and a willingness to make common cause with other Churches in the work of witnessing to the action of God in the world. A consequence of this is the opportunity which ecumenism offers for the Churches to work together in the promotion of moral value. The Christian Churches, as we have already had occasion to notice, differ among themselves upon some items of morality out of their common heritage, but they have a great deal more in common and there is much scope for common effort in pursuit of their common mission.

For the Churches exist not, so to speak, for themselves, but as sent into the world to proclaim the Good News of salvation. The Church is mission, as it is usual to say nowadays, and its *raison d'être* is to witness to what was accomplished by God in Jesus and the Spirit. So it stands in the 'world' with a message, addressed to successive generations and to all cultures. Is it therefore over against the world, in constant confrontation with the world's values, a light shining in the darkness, but for which the world would go astray? What is 'the world'?

In looking at the Roman Catholic Church's understanding of itself today we shall see that one of the characteristics of that understanding is the increasing prominence accorded to the layperson. It is a simplification, though not unfair, to say that prior to the Council the prevailing model of the Church was of an institution in which the roles of leaders and led were sharply separated, with the latter category in a decidedly subservient place. But the Council made it plain that every member has her or his own vocation, and the lay member of the Church is gradually being accorded a greater recognition, in theory if not always in practice and even if, as many think, too slowly. One field in which this development is having effect is that of the exercise of authority. Not that the principle of hierarchical authority has come in question, but the manner of its exercise is in process of change. An authority which understands itself as one of service is bound to differ in its style from one conceived as lordship. The character of the authority and its scope have also been receiving attention. For instance, one of the modern emphases is upon the irreplaceability of lay (as distinct from clerical and especially hierarchical) experience, and the Council spoke of an 'autonomy of earthly affairs'. Put simply this means that the cleric as such is not an expert in (say) politics, and it is not for him to seek to tell the politicians how to do their job. We shall be seeing something of what these developments import for the exercise of authority in the context of our concerns.

This is a convenient point at which to clarify a matter of terminology. I have already referred to a tendency in the public mind to equate the Churches with their leaderships, and it is probably true to say that in no Church is this tendency more marked than in my own. The Second Vatican Council went to some trouble to underline the fact that the Church is the whole 'People of God', and for a time it was almost a fashion to make a point of saying that 'the Church is not just the pope and the bishops'. The fashion has however passed and it is again common, even in official documents, to use 'Church' to refer to those who hold *magisterium* or authoritative teaching competence.

Whatever the fashion of usage, the truth is that the Church may not be equated with its *magisterium,* and a usage which continues to do this is wrong. Up to now in these pages, in an effort to avoid this mistake, I have spoken of church 'leadership'. But of course leadership in the Catholic Church is exercised by people other than the pope and the bishops; and from now on, in the absence of a special reason for doing otherwise, I shall use the old-fashioned and perhaps unattractive but accurate word hierarchy in reference to the holders of the offices we have here in mind.

Against this backdrop we come eventually to the focal preoccupation of the book: how is the Catholic to vote in matters of morality and law? As indicated, I shall submit that a framework for addressing this question is supplied by the teaching of the *Declaration on Religious Freedom* of Vatican Two. The teaching of the Declaration refers of course to freedom of religious belief and practice, and it is not self-evident that it may be applied to moral matters as well; and its applicability will have to be argued for explicitly. I hope to show that the import of the transfer of the Declaration's teaching to the moral sphere is that in principle Catholics are in the same position as anyone else when it comes to the question of embodying a moral belief in the law. I shall, in other words, be maintaining that for Catholics, no less and no more than for others, the question always is one of reconciling individual freedom with the requirements of a common good.

But that is not the end of the matter, for there are different ways of envisaging this task and there are differences of viewpoint as to what the common good might in a given case require. In very broad terms one might say that there are two approaches, one whose main emphasis is on the value of individual freedom, another whose ultimate point of reference is a societal conception of good. These approaches were reflected in a celebrated debate between Sir Patrick (now Lord) Devlin and the then Professor of Jurisprudence at Oxford, H.L.A. Hart. A review of their discussions may help us see our own positions mirrored, each side portrayed lucidly and with authority. The crux is the question, what are the criteria for legislation involving the enforcement of morals? I hope to show that there are some criteria which, while not providing instant answers, may help a community and its legislators decide.

How *should* a Catholic vote? Neither Hart nor Devlin provides a specifically Catholic formula, and Catholics must join with others in trying to balance the claims of individual liberty and those of a common good. And there are no easy answers, and no escaping a conscientious effort to come to a conclusion in each particular case. But if there is no one Catholic answer, Catholics have been among the thinkers whose reflections supply pointers which others as well as Catholics may find helpful in making up their minds. The work of the American Jesuit John Courtney Murray remains authoritative, and the current US debate is contributing a continuing clarification.

In that debate one question in particular is the object of a special scrutiny. Geraldine Ferraro's reply to a query as to her intentions regarding the law on abortion seemed to echo a response of John F. Kennedy to a comparable question. Yet it fuelled an ongoing controversy, and the controversy has probed the adequacy of the distinction between the personal moral belief and the public stance of the office-holder. It will be argued here that the distinction remains valid, for all that it is sometimes blandly made. It is a merit of the debate to have forced a more nuanced account of it.

The Catholic Church has a social mission; it wishes its message to influence public affairs. That fact is enough to give special point to the question how its members are expected to vote. The freedom which is argued for here may leave a believer uneasy: is it selling the message short? The critic will be sceptical: how, granted its mission, can the Church *not* have designs on the minds of those whom it addresses? Is to keep it out of the public forum the only hope?

The separation of Church and State is not the removal of Church from society; wherever religious freedom is acknowledged room is made for a Church's presence, a right of audience granted its voice. But if the voice is to be heard today the presence must be credible. And style of address and idiom as well as content must be appropriate to our time.

2

WHAT BEING MORAL MEANS

Morality may be described as the art of right relationship with each other and with the world around us. The use of the word 'art' may at first sight be puzzling and its choice will be explained in due course. But first we should look at the other elements in the description.

Relationship is a fundamental feature of being human. We come into the world as the fruit of the relationship of our parents and even for survival we need from the outset to be in some kind of sustaining relationship with another. In normal circumstances a child is in dependent relationship first to parents, and he or she comes to maturity in a network of relationships which contribute to nurturing and education in a complex variety of ways.

At first our relationships are non-reflective, some of them even unconscious; spontaneously we just *are*—children or sisters or brothers or pupils or friends, or a doctor's patients or a barber's customers. But as we grow in self-awareness we become aware of our relationships, and gradually we become aware of being able to make some choices in their regard. I cannot change the fact that I am a child of X and Y, but I find that I have some control over the way in which I behave towards them. I cannot avoid being in the relationship of classmate to Z, but I can choose whether or not I want Z for a friend.

Understanding and Choice

These two characteristics of the human being, awareness and a capacity for choice, are the foundation of morality. For awareness tells us something about the way the world is, and our capacity for choice allows us to decide how we are going to conduct ourselves in it. A more familiar way of putting this, perhaps, is to say that humans are knowing and free, and that their knowledge and freedom are the basis for morality.

Not that our knowledge is often full and clear, or our freedom ever absolutely pure. We can forget, make mistakes, are sometimes ignorant of truth; and sometimes our judgment is clouded by excess of emotion or by factors deep in our psychology of which we may not even be conscious. Our freedom is always bounded by our knowledge, and it may be trammelled too by compulsions and fears and other stirrings of the psyche, including, again, forces within us of which we may not even be aware.

Our knowledge and our freedom are invariably affected also by our environment. This may be seen in an obvious way when we look at, say, a child from a broken home in a deprived urban environment. He or she may not know right from wrong simply because they have never been taught, either at home or at school (for of course these are where moral rules and values are normally mainly learned). Or they may have been taught in a nominal sense, but the values or rules may not have registered—perhaps because of a discrepancy between what they hear and what they see others do. Or indeed what has been taught may have registered, but a social pressure seems nevertheless to drive them to steal or maim or take drugs.

That kind of illustration of the influence of the environment is commonplace, but we need not think that environmental or peer-group pressure is confined to those whom we consider deprived. Moral sensibility may be imperilled also in settings which we should consider privileged: as when the context in which I live precludes my seeing dole-queues or the effects of emigration, and I remain untroubled by the inequities in our society of which these are symptoms. Any of us may be blinded by the prejudices of our background so that we are deprived of the capacity to recognise and respond to certain kinds of good and evil.

Yet normally we have sufficient knowledge and capacity for choice to be able in some fashion to direct our lives. The recognition that we are always influenced by our makeup or our environment has not persuaded people to abandon the language of praise or blame, or to cease to try to change our ways or encourage others to change theirs. Which is to say that people generally hold on to the idea of moral *responsibility*—to the idea that we are able to make something of ourselves and our world, and that we are answerable for what we make of ourselves and how.

So the dimension of experience which we call morality is founded on our capacity to know and to choose: these characteristics of the human are what enable us to practise the art of relating to other people and to our world. But the description with which we are working mentions 'right', and the idea of morality includes the notion that there is right and a wrong way of relating.

Right or Wrong, Good or Bad?

Right and wrong in terms of what? We may for the moment think of right as meaning conformity with a standard or rule: with being just, for example, as required by a rule that we should be just; or giving money to a poor person, in accordance with a principle that we should give alms; or refraining from stealing, according to the precept that we ought not to steal. But why these rules, or where did they come from, and why should we conform to them?

We might answer this by reflecting that another way of putting what we have just been saying is that it is 'good' to be just, or to give alms, and 'evil' or 'bad' to steal. Speaking very strictly, the terms right and wrong, even in a moral context, are mainly descriptive of compliance or otherwise with some standard; though inevitably there is also a suggestion of commendation or disapproval of whatever or whomever is said to be right or wrong. With the expressions good and evil this evaluative ingredient comes into prominence: a good radio is to be prized and praised, as is a good read; and a good person makes as it were a demand upon our regard.

A good person? It is not hard to judge whether a radio is good or bad, or a book—or indeed a singer or football player or student. For it is not difficult to find criteria by which these judgments may be made, even if people differ sometimes as to the precise criteria, or how they are to be ranked, or how exactly applied. But a good person? Following a classical philosophical tradition and adapting the OED we could say that we call a thing good when it is what it was called to be. So a person is good when he or she is what he or she *is* called to be. 'Call' is figurative; a religious person may think here of the call of God, but the expression need mean no more than that a particular way of being or acting is according to our nature.

And what is that? Several answers are possible. If what characterises the human person are the twin gifts of reason and freedom, we are what we are called to be when exercising our freedom rationally. And that indeed is an apt description of what being moral means. But it is abstract and general, and people are more attracted by a somewhat warmer way of putting it; and more than one religious or philosophical tradition would be happy with the proposition that human beings are called to love.

Love is a troublesome word of course, its meaning confused in the variety of its usage. A child loves ice-cream as well as his parents, a whole generation loved the Rolling Stones, Dante loved Beatrice, and

J.R. loved many women. C.S. Lewis wrote a book called *The Four Loves*, from which it may be seen that even when we use the word aptly we may be talking of different forms. But there is at least the residue of a core meaning, and for present purposes we can say that love means wishing people well and doing them good.

So the good person is one who loves. But this too is general, and we need immediately to give it concrete content. We could say that to love is to appreciate another, to have regard (in more than one sense); and to express this appreciation and regard in our dispositions and attitudes and intentions and actions. We should therefore acknowledge the dignity of others, respect their life and person, aim to do them good, be just and truthful, don't steal from them or take away their good name, refrain from harming them in any way.

Moral Rules

These are some of the 'rules' of morality, and they follow from the nature of the enterprise, and the nature of the enterprise is determined by our nature as human beings. Humans are called to love, and the 'precepts' or 'commandments' which are a feature of all moral systems are simply statements of a standard or test of loving.

It may be noticed, incidentally, that the rules listed by way of illustration above are of differing kinds. Some are general: acknowledge the dignity of others, respect their life and person, aim to do good. Others are more specific: be just and truthful, don't steal or defame. Of both general and specific some have to do in the first place with states of mind (acknowledgment of dignity, respect, a will to do good, a disposition to justice)—which is why earlier when speaking of the content of loving I mentioned, as well as action, an *internal* dimension comprised of factors such as disposition, attitude and intention. This is an important point, for we need to grasp that morality is not just external conformity with rules. Eliot's Becket expresses a persistent ethical theme when he reflects that 'the greatest treason [is]/ to do the right deed for the wrong reason'.

But where do the rules come from? Most immediately they come from the moral tradition of the community into which each of us is born. Tradition refers both to a process of handing on and to *what* is handed on, and a moral tradition in the second sense consists in the values and principles and rules which comprise the 'code' of the community. Normally it is handed on through the usual educational processes, formal and informal, at home or in school or church, or through other educational agencies of society. In our time the media of social communication are potent agents of the transmission of moral value, good and bad: think of the effect of a television documentary about famine in Ethiopia, or the power of a clever advertisement.

A word on terminology may be in order at this point again. The code just referred to is not necessarily something written; it is used here to designate in shorthand the ensemble of values and principles and rules in the light of which a community lives or aspires to live its life. A 'value' is something that is prized, considered to be important: in a moral context because of the bearing which it has on human flourishing. Life is a value, as are honour and honesty and the keeping of promises. Communities or families usually rank values—though not always consciously—in a certain order of priority, and by both teaching and example they try to communicate these to the next generation.

This means, among other things, expressing the values in the form of 'principles' or 'rules', which are intended to guide our actions so that the value is 'realised'. We have seen examples of some of these already. The value of life, for instance, is recognised in the principle that human life ought to be respected and in the rule that we ought not to kill. The former of these is general, giving a general shape to our activities but not on its face saying anything concerning concrete action. The second is concrete, referring to a particular piece of activity. Both kinds are necessary in guiding our lives: the first gives moral meaning to the second, the second helps translate the first into practice.

Notice that the second is also negative in form—it is a prohibition. Now the picture which many people have of morality is of a list of prohibitions: though we sometimes refer to moral precepts as ' do's and don'ts', we seem to find it easier to think of examples of the don'ts. No doubt this is partly explained by the fact that the kind of moral education which most got was negatively cast: thou shalt not kill, commit adultery, steal, lie, lust, and so on. But perhaps it is in some sense natural to latch on to prohibitions, especially those which are concrete. For one thing they have a relative clarity—each refers to a definite type of action or state of affairs or state of mind. And each helps mark off what is nowadays called the bottom line, so that we are clear at least on morality's minimal demands. This type of rule resembles that which requires that a sailing boat is not brought too close to the wind. It is not the perfection of sailing, but at least the boat doesn't stop.

These prohibitions have an irreplaceable function, for it is important to be able to mark off the bottom line; but they are not the whole of morality. There is a good deal more to respect for life than refraining from killing people, and truthfulness is more than not telling lies. Doing justice is more than not stealing, and there are many ways in which a man might fail in faithfulness to his wife apart from adultery or beating her up. A moral education which restricts itself to prohibitions gives an impoverished sense of morals and a minimalist conception of what it is to be a human being. This will turn out to be an important point when we come to consider the enforcement of morality by law.

We have just noticed two types of rule or principle, one general, the other more concrete. In the language of the study of ethics the first type is often called *formal,* the second *material,* and it will be useful for us to recall these terms later. A third type of principle is exemplified in the statement that 'murder is wrong'. This is a tautology, for murder in moral discourse *means* 'wrongful killing'. Tautologous principles have their uses, though they are sometimes used misleadingly in place of material ones. Again it will be helpful later to remember this term.

In ethical writing the terms 'principle' and 'rule', together with 'norm' and 'commandment', and 'precept' and 'imperative' tend to be used interchangeably, and I shall use them interchangeably here in the absence of a particular reason for making a distinction. But perhaps one may say that the words commandment, precept and imperative, though used synonymously with the others, possess or at least accentuate an additional nuance. For these words bring out the sense of *obligation* which is a feature of our understanding of morality. We do not think of being just or truthful or fairminded as merely a good idea; rather we think of these things as somehow *demanded* of us. Demanded by whom and why?

Why be Moral?

Earlier when we asked ourselves where moral rules come from we saw that in the most obvious sense they come from the tradition of the community. Now, again obviously, we can see that the demand that we keep the rules comes from the community, concretely mediated through parents, teachers, peers, society. But where did the community get the rules, and why should it ask us to keep them? It is worth pursuing these questions a little. One of the chief reasons why people—especially the young—resist moral rules is that they reject the authority of whomever they perceive to be imposing them.

Some readers will no doubt be surprised that I do not now adduce God as the author of moral rules (What about the Ten Commandments? The Sermon on the Mount?), and His will as the basis of our obligation to keep them. For many people see morality in exactly this way: as God's law which must be kept because He said so, and because He will punish or reward us, depending upon the measure of our compliance. The reason I do not adduce God as the author of the rules of morality is that He is not their author *in this sense* at all. And harm is done both to our notion of God and to our grasp of morality when we conceive His connection with morality in this way. We shall be seeing more of all this later.

But where do the rules come from, and why obey them? Their author is the human mind, reflecting on human experience, discovering what is or is not fit living for a creature with a human nature. This discovery is always in process, for there is no end to change in the conditions of our living, and the change forces us to a ceaseless search for the right way for humans to live. There are of course some constants: we are body-spirits, with minds and hearts and will; rational and free, as the philosophers have it. We are sexual beings with an instinct for the reproduction of our kind. We need food, clothing and shelter. And these constants generate certain general requirements of human flourishing, which is another way of saying that the general requirements of morality do not change. But their concrete application varies, and we are never freed from the quest for the right way.

I have used the expression 'human flourishing' in reference to the point of being moral; an older expression is 'human fulfilment', older still (but perhaps misleading) the word 'happiness'. What is in question is the idea that the point of anything is that it should *be* in the way which best suits the kind of thing it is: that things always aim at the 'perfection' of whatever their nature is. And the perfection of a human nature is in the direction of rational choice—or of loving, if you prefer that way of putting it. Humans flourish inasmuch as they exercise their freedom according to the claims of reality, or again, more warmly, when they truly love.

The foregoing is no more than a fairly standard account of what Catholic theology has meant by the doctrine of natural law. And we shall see that the concept is enhanced, though not in substance altered, in the light of Christian beliefs about ultimate human destiny. There have been theological objections to it of course: notably the Lutheran one that it makes too much of both nature and reason, ignoring the radical damage to humanity which is expressed in the notion of the Fall. Other critics think that there are so many problems about the idea of a 'law of nature', especially when it purports to prescribe unvarying moral demands, that it is not seriously serviceable as an account of the basis of morality now. Yet the essential ingredients of the doctrine of natural law have proved difficult to dispense with and it remains central, albeit in newer versions—and sometimes in disguise—in most Catholic moral theology still.

✓Of course some think that the point of being moral is simply survival: that the demands of morality originated and have their justification in the concrete conditions of the persistence of individuals and of the species. But does this accord with our experience? It may well be that historically the first perceptions of, say, the value of life were self-interested, and that what came to be called the Golden Rule was at first no more than the insight that it is expedient to live and let live. And no doubt we often do what is right from self-interest rather than from nobler motives. But we are never content for long with this version of things. We are not content with mere survival but are drawn to a certain 'quality' in our living. In the context of our relationships that quality includes attitudes such as gentleness and compassion and unselfishness. It calls us sometimes to turn the other cheek or go the second mile; and it asks some to lay down their life for their friend. Such manifestations of the flourishing of humanity are not explicable in terms of the requirements of survival merely.

Moral rules come to us out of the tradition of the community, but their ultimate origin is in the race's attempt to make sense of its experience; or, if you like, in human reason reflecting on human nature. And we ought, therefore, to obey the rules not just as it were on the say-so of the community or its authorities but because and to the extent that they indicate the way of human flourishing. The answer to the question, why be moral? is not because society or the Church or even God requires it, but that it is through being moral that we become truly human.

God and Morals

This account of the origin of morality and the basis of moral obligation is intelligible to people other than religious believers, and in discussion with nonbelievers it is obviously preferable to an account couched in religious language. But that is not its only value, and at least as important is the fact that it gives morality its own independent weight. When moral right and wrong are seen as based exclusively on a command of God, they are in danger of being seen as merely extrinsically imposed, and our grasp of morality's meaning is thereby impoverished. For then its significance for the flourishing of our nature is likely be obscured, and it is seen as alien rather than congenial to us. And so we submit to (or resist) its claims, not in understanding and freedom but more or less blindly, in a way best described as infantile.

When the command of God is linked with promise of reward or threat of punishment, so that we obey out of fear or in the hope of winning approval, our motivation too is debased. Human motives are rarely pure in any case; but if we are moved to be just or truthful solely for fear of the consequences of acting otherwise, we have as it were missed the point of morality altogether. Truthfulness or justice have their own intrinsic worth, and they should be pursued for what they are worth in themselves. A view of morality which of its nature precludes our seeing them thus is a falsification.

But though God is not the author of morality's rules in the crude sense which it is all too easy to take from some attempts to relate religion and morality, it by no means follows that He has no connection with morality at all. For the Bible teaches that God *is* the author of the creation, and that He has made humans in His own likeness. It is in the creativity of the human being that morality originates; but Christian theology sees that creativity as reflecting and indeed expressing the creativity of God. This is what St Thomas Aquinas had in mind when he wrote of natural law as a 'sharing in the Eternal Law by rational creatures'.[1]

An account of morality in secular terms should not leave the Christian disquieted for it is the consequence of a deeply theological insight.[2] It enhances morality by pointing up its intrinsic worth. But it also enhances religion, by freeing it to achieve its true breadth and depth. Of course we should expect religious faith to have something to say to morality. For how we relate to the world and each other depends on what we make of life, and what we make of life is expressed in our 'faith' or other world-view. The Christian faith is a way of looking at life, and it is not surprising that as such it should have something to say to questions about how we are to live. Later we shall look in some detail at the ways in which the Christian faith illuminates the practice of morality. But it is worth emphasising that even on a classical Christian view it is possible to give an account of morality without recourse to religious terms.

An Art?
The description with which this chapter began spoke of morality as an art, and now it is time to explain why. The word is apposite for it is suggestive at several levels. Its most basic sense is of a skill which comes from knowledge and practice,[3] and we have seen enough to appreciate how morality might be described as an art in this sense. Plainly it

requires a knowledge, an ensemble of notions and values and principles which express in the concrete the requirements of the good life. But the good life is to be *lived,* not just known or appreciated in the abstract. Moral knowledge is for putting into *practice* and the practice both expresses and reinforces our ideas about how we are meant to live.

The word 'art' is suggestive in another way, for it also intimates a performance or achievement which is more than the simple application of a rule. There are principles of musical composition, for example, but the art of Beethoven is more than his observance of these rules. One could say, I suppose, that among the things which make us regard him as a great composer is the way in which he 'works with' the rules, fashioning in music his vision. Vision in this context is not (if it ever is) something of the mind only; music too is, as Wordsworth said of poetry, felt in the blood and felt along the heart.[4] And, as in poetry or music, moral sensibility includes an engagement of the imagination which allows us to see into the life of things.[5]

Justice, as Aristotle said, is not merely the doing of just actions, but the doing of them in the way of the just person.[6] That means behaving out of a right intention and motive and attitude, and a general disposition to justice. And a disposition to justice or any other form of goodness, translated into practice, leads to a certain ease of performance. Someone who possesses the appropriate 'art' will be observed to play golf or to sing or paint with a kind of fluency. And so it is with morals: disposition translates into habit, and habit tends towards facility, and we develop a 'style'. In this sense too, therefore, we might speak of an art of good living.

There is a fourth reason for conceiving of good living as an art. It is that the best achievements of the artist are sometimes experienced by him or her (and perceived by others) as somehow 'given', as it were from outside. People speak of being 'taken over', 'possessed', 'inspired', so that their performance—as painter, actor, footballer—exceeds in excellence what they had thought to be their potential. This too may happen in the moral life: there are times in which we appear to transcend ourselves, to be more courageous or loving or truthful than is 'natural' for us; and we may aptly speak of having been 'gifted'. The religious person will think of the concept of grace, which imports the notion of gift from God, as well as empowering and enhancement.

Morality and Law

The foregoing exploration of the meaning of morality has attended to aspects which are important for the purposes of this book. But the aspect which is focal for our concerns is morality's relationship with law and it is to this that we now turn. Of course morality itself is often called the moral law, but the law now in question is that made as it were 'additionally' by those who have the care of a community: positive law, as it is sometimes called, from a Latin word meaning to lay down.

This law is there because it was enacted by a lawmaker in some sense of that expression, or perhaps because it grew out of custom. In modern experience it is usually written, and its precepts are to be found in constitutions and charters and statute-books and in some systems in the decisions of judges. There are understandable reasons for referring to morality as the moral law, but for clarity I shall continue to prefer the term morality in reference to those demands imposed on us not in the first place by decision of a lawmaker or by custom but by our nature as rational and free beings.

Morality and law resemble each other, and in some matters their scopes overlap, and the resemblances and overlap are a potent source of confusion. It will be helpful now to compare and contrast them, with an eye to features of each which are of special interest in view of the theme of this book.

Morality and law resemble each other. Each has to do with the regulation of human behaviour, each deals in rules which enjoin or prohibit certain acts or omissions or states of affairs. Morality requires that we respect human life, the law that we drive on a particular side of the road. It is morally wrong to drive in a way which endangers life, it is illegal to exceed the speed limit in a built-up area. And both morality and law *oblige* us in a way which we recognise as more cogent than the force of convention or etiquette or taste. Only in an attenuated sense are we obliged to use a fish-knife, and no-one is compelled to read Shakespeare, unless by way of having to comply with, say, the requirements of a course in English literature.

In some matters the scopes of law and morality overlap. They both forbid murder, perjury and theft, to name but three of the items which come within the purview of each. They intersect in another sense too, for law requires the support of morality, and aspects of morality may be expressed in law; and morality normally requires that we obey the law. To drive at sixty miles an hour in a residential area full of children can hardly be other than crassly immoral as well as a breach of the speed limit.

But morality and law differ too, and the differences are profoundly important. For one thing—a point which we have glimpsed already—they differ in their origins: the one has its roots in our nature, the other in a lawmaker's *fiat*. Relatedly, the source of obligation of each is different: the exigencies of human flourishing, and the will of a ruler or whomever is the bearer of authority in the *polis*.

Another difference between law and morality is that the latter always pays attention to internal factors such as one's disposition or attitude or intention, whereas a good deal of law does not. From the law's point of view it doesn't matter with what sense of resentment I pay my taxes; if I pay them I have complied with the law. But from a moral point of view resentment may mar what is ostensibly correct; as when I do a good turn with bad grace. If I wrong someone inadvertently I cannot be blamed morally, since I didn't mean to do so. But if inadvertently I exceed the speed limit or fail to pay my TV licence I can only hope for the indulgence of policeman or judge, for I stand liable to punishment, having broken, unquestionably, the law. An incidental implication is that compliance with the law is no guarantee of moral worth.

And indeed morality may require that we disobey a law. Normally we are morally obliged to keep the law of the land, and it is morally wrong to do what is illegal. Laws are laid down in aid of community welfare, and compliance with them is usually one of the preconditions of human flourishing. But a law may be immoral, as when it discriminates unfairly on the basis of race or religion or sex. A law may enjoin an immorality, as in Hitler's Germany in relation to Jews. From a moral standpoint it will not do to excuse ourselves by saying 'I obeyed the law'; and for all that normally we are morally obliged to keep the law there may be times when we are obliged to disobey.

A Higher Law?

This last theme is as old as Antigone, yet as fresh in the memory as the Nürnberg trials after the Second World War. Antigone buried her brother Polynices, defying an order made by Creon, king of Thebes, who had forbidden him honourable burial. In Sophocles' play, she defends herself by appeal to a higher law.

> That order did not come from God. Justice
> That dwells with the gods below, knows no such law.
> I did not think your edicts strong enough
> To overrule the unwritten unalterable laws
> Of God and heaven, you being only a man.
> They are not of yesterday or today, but everlasting,
> Though where they came from, none of us can tell.[7]

The notion of a higher law to which all, even rulers, are answerable, has persisted in western thinking in the form of some version of the doctrine of 'Natural Law'. Not that all versions of the doctrine have come to the same thing, and no version has escaped criticism. Yet commentators have seen some such notion at work even in the ostensibly positivist[8] climate of the Nürnberg Tribunal for the trial of war crimes. 'An order is an order', the accused officials pleaded, meaning that they were obliged to do what was commanded by political and military superiors and were thus justified in what they had done. But the plea did not succeed; and A.P. d'Entrèves has written, 'The rejection of the defence of superior orders . . . is nothing less than the old doctrine that the validity of laws does not depend on their "positiveness", and that it is the duty of the individual to pass judgment on laws before he obeys them'.[9]

So although morality and law are in some ways alike, and are interrelated and interdependent, the differences between them are radical. The one is not the other, nor can either take the other's place. It is wrong to expect too much of the law: to think that it can make us morally good, to confuse legality with virtue. A propensity to legislate instead of to educate inhibits moral growth.

Yet it would be wrong to discount law's role in assisting the promotion of moral value. St Thomas had a high idea of its place: he included it among the ways in which God 'educates' us in goodness. His account of how this happens is, as we shall see, nuanced, and his expectations of law were modest. Yet he is clear that it has a role. 'From becoming accustomed to shun what is evil and discharge what is good on account of threat of punishment a man sometimes comes to continue on that course from his own taste and choice. Hence law even as punitive brings men to good.'[10] Our time is familiar with the use of law in the securing of rights, at domestic as well as international level. Laws which counter racial discrimination in the United States, for example, or which in Ireland promote equal opportunity in the employment of women, embody moral insights which, it may be hoped, in time will come to flourish of their own accord.

When comparing and contrasting morality and law we noticed that in some matters their scopes overlap, and that they are interrelated and indeed interdependent; and H.L.A. Hart has listed the main questions which may be put about this. The first is whether the development of law has been influenced by morals (and vice versa), the second whether some reference to morality enters into an adequate definition of law. A third asks whether the law is open to moral criticism, and the fourth is whether it is the business of the law to enforce morality—more exactly, to make immorality a crime.[11]

The second and third have often been debated by moralists and jurisprudents, notably in discussion of the relative merits of legal positivism and natural law theory; we have just seen a practical illustration of their significance in our allusion to the Nürnberg trials. The fourth has long been associated with the name of John Stuart Mill, though nowadays it is more likely to evoke the names of Devlin and Hart, and it focuses the concerns of this book.

But it is well to remember that it is only one of the questions which may be put, and indeed some may think that it is not the most important. At any rate it cannot be treated in isolation from the others, and though we cannot cope in detail with all aspects of the relationships between law and morality I shall try to keep them in mind and we shall advert to them as may incidentally be necessary.

3

MORALITY AND THE CHRISTIAN FAITH

In looking at morality as the art of right relationship with each other and the world around us we saw that it is a natural accompaniment of human living. It may be accounted for without reference to religious belief and indeed there are many people who subscribe to and achieve a high moral standard without being committed to a religious faith in any usual sense. But Christian faith sheds light on the moral life, and in this chapter we look more closely at how this is so.

Perhaps the best point of entry is by way of relevant biblical material, for the Bible is the source and reference point *par excellence* for Christian theologising. According to Roman Catholic tradition, 'the divinely revealed realities which are contained and presented in the text of Sacred Scripture have been written down under the inspiration of the Holy Spirit'.[1] But even for those who do not see the Bible in this light, its books are the formative and normative expression of the Judaeo-Christian religious heritage. Its perspectives and emphases no less than its explicit teaching remain instructive in the shaping of theology in our time.

Two Questions

Two questions will be of particular interest to us. The first is the general question of what was made of morality during the formative phase of the Church, the second the more particular question of the relationship between the Church and the civil power. But from the outset it is important to place these questions in context. It is a basic theme of this book that the primary work of the Church is to bear witness to a gospel of human salvation; and all its other concerns, including its concern with morality, are in aid of that witness. This is evident from even the most rudimentary summary of the biblical data.

The Context

The Christian religion is founded upon the belief that God is disclosed uniquely in Jesus Christ. According to a modern theological emphasis that disclosure took place in the personal *history* of Jesus; as the Constitution on Revelation of the Second Vatican Council has it, Jesus revealed God 'by the total fact of his presence and self-manifestation— by words and works, signs and miracles, but above all by his death and glorious resurrection from the dead, and finally by sending the Spirit of truth'.[2] What this means is that God is disclosed, and His design for His creation, in the detail of the personal history of Jesus.

That history itself took place within the history of a people who had already experienced themselves as especially chosen. God, they believed, was already revealing Himself in the unfolding story of their 'deliver- ance' in accordance with a promise which He made to Abraham and ratified in a covenant with Moses. Although their expectations were in time no longer crassly political, most of them were unprepared for the claim that their deliverance was less from temporal enemies and evils than from the bondage of sin, and that their saviour was a travelling rabbi from Nazareth who said he was the Son of God.

So they crucified him, but 'God raised him up',[3] and later he was seen by some of the disciples.[4] Later again they came to recognise that he had left them definitively and had gone back to the Father.[5] And then what came to be called the Church was born in the coming together of Jesus' disciples, following his injunction to remember in the breaking of bread[6] what he had done, or what God had done in him. The core of the disciples' belief was that Jesus was Lord, who had died and was risen and would some time come again. They were at first fearful and inhibited but, transformed by the Pentecost event, at length went forth to tell others of their faith and hope.[7]

Their message was called 'good news'—the Greek *euangelion* and the English 'gospel' have comparable roots. In classical Greek the term was often used in reference to the announcement of a victory, and in a religious context it could signify a divine utterance. But the sense in which the expression came most readily to the disciples was a strictly biblical one: it echoed exactly a word used in Second Isaiah to signify that the time of salvation was at hand.

Salvation was a familiar theme in the religious patrimony of Israel. The complex history of the theme is beyond our purpose; essentially the concept signified the action of God in the life of the chosen people in virtue of which they were to achieve the destiny promised the descendants of Abraham. The shape of that destiny disclosed itself only gradually, and only gradually did it come to be associated with the expectation of a messiah. But by the time of the prophets it had begun to appear that salvation was primarily in the spiritual order, and the saviour was seen in the role of a suffering Servant.[8]

This was the backdrop to the events which are the subject of the narratives which we now call gospels. These books, each from its own viewpoint, document the impact of Jesus of Nazareth upon his first hearers. They tell the story of Jesus, a story which was perceived by himself and by those who became his disciples as continuing and completing the story of God's dealings with the people of His choice.

And so Luke portrays Jesus early in his public ministry announcing in the synagogue at Nazareth that the words of the prophet Isaiah were that day fulfilled: 'The Spirit of the Lord is upon me, because he has anointed me to preach good news to the poor. He has sent me to proclaim release to the captives and recovering of sight to the blind, to set at liberty those who are oppressed, to proclaim the acceptable year of the Lord'.[9] That *this* is the salvation which Israel was waiting for was a main theme in the spreading of the good news.

It seems that a brief telling of the story of Jesus was a central feature in the early proclamation of the gospel. Several of Paul's letters and some passages in the Acts of the Apostles incorporate such a narrative, and Peter's speech to Cornelius as reported in Acts will serve to exemplify this here.

> You know the word which [God] sent to Israel, preaching the good news of peace by Jesus Christ (he is Lord of all), the word which was proclaimed throughout all Judaea, beginning from Galilee after the baptism which John preached: how God anointed Jesus of Nazareth with the Holy Spirit and with power; how he went about doing good and healing all that were oppressed by the devil, for God was with him. And we are witnesses to all that he did both in the country of the Jews and in Jerusalem. They put him to death by hanging him on a tree; but God raised him on the third day and made him manifest; not to all the people but to us who were chosen by God as witnesses, who ate and drank with him after he rose from the dead. And he commanded us to preach to the people, and to testify that he is the one ordained by God to be judge of the living and the dead. To him all the prophets bear witness that everyone who believes in him receives forgiveness of sins through his name.[10]

So we have a community—or, more exactly, communities—gathering in remembrance of the story of Jesus' life, and especially in what would come to be known as the paschal events; and then going out to spread the word that in him is salvation accomplished. It took a little time before the new 'Churches' realised their distinctiveness in the common Jewish tradition, a little longer before it was clear that subscription to that tradition was not a prerequisite of entry into the Christian 'way'. And it took yet longer before their community of faith and worship generated a community of organisation: before, that is, the Churches became the Church, which in time would be one in government as well as in worship and faith.

But from the outset the Churches saw themselves as charged with proclaiming the good news. The disciples were conscious of being 'sent', as Peter's speech just quoted shows. Matthew records a sending,[11] and later he presents the risen Lord on a mountain in Galilee bidding the eleven 'go and make disciples of all nations, baptising them in the name of the Father and of the Son and of the Holy Spirit, teaching them to observe all that I have commanded you'.[12]

It is a commonplace of modern ecclesiology that the Church 'is mission'—so much a commonplace that one is tempted to try to find another way of saying what is meant. Yet there is hardly a more exact way of saying that in its very coming together to celebrate Jesus as Lord it is meant to go forth to affirm what it celebrates. 'As the Father has sent me I also send you.'[13] In a later theological perspective the Church would be seen as a visible expression in history of the saving work of Christ.

An Ethical Religion

It is time now to turn to the first of the questions in which we must be especially interested: what was made of morality itself in the formative phase of the Church. The Christian religion, wrote C.H. Dodd, 'is an ethical religion in the specific sense that it recognises no ultimate separation between the service of God and social behaviour'.[14] What this means is that you cannot claim to love the God of Jesus Christ unless you love the neighbour. Of course the link between religion and morality had already been affirmed in Judaism, and there was much in the tradition inherited by the first Christians to remind them of it. V. Warnach has summarised the data: 'In the Old Testament the love which God bestows upon men, above all on the chosen people, is for the most part understood as faithfulness to the covenant. In view of this it is not surprising that the reciprocal love of men should likewise be conceived of as consisting essentially in the acceptance of covenant obligations'.[15]

These obligations included worship; but no less did they stress the need for a right relationship with the neighbour. And indeed it was to be a constant theme, especially in the preaching of the prophets, that the God of Israel was not placated by mere ritual in the absence of a conversion of heart expressed in right conduct toward others.[16]

And so it was not as it were out of the blue that Jesus preached repentance. 'Repentance' translates a Greek word *metanoia* which is much richer in its signification than the English. Its chief Old Testament antecedent is a Hebrew word *shuv*, whose literal meaning is to return to the place from which one has set out—that is to God. When Jesus called for repentance he was calling on people to turn about, to re-orientate their lives, to make a fresh beginning, to go back to God.[17]

Yet the call to repentance was not the primary motif of the message; that motif was, rather, the coming of the kingdom of God. Again we must be careful of the English word: 'kingship' or 'reign' or 'rule' are better guides to the biblical sense. For in the tradition God had often been thought of as king, and in time the hope of Israel was expressed in terms of the setting up of his kingly rule in Israel and among the nations.[18] But the rule would not be a merely political dominion. Isaiah's vision of it is summarised by Rudolf Schnackenburg: 'The peace of paradise will be brought back (Is.11:6-9), and, in general, this kingdom of God fulfilled in the last age takes on universal characteristics even though Israel has always the place of honour. It also has cosmic dimensions and a clearly religious and moral character—salvation and peace and the law established as the basis of the world order.'[19] It will simplify matters if we indicate its meaning by calling it the universal reign of God's love.

In Jesus' preaching the advent of that reign is the context of the call to repentance. Mark's portrayal of the opening of the public ministry shows this:'The time is fulfilled and the kingdom of God is at hand; repent, and believe in the gospel.'[20] The time of the promise is here, the rule of God's love is inaugurated, and the people are called to turn again to him. The turning implies a change of heart, the change is expressed in walking along the right path. But the turning is in another sense only like a first move, a step within a larger process. For Jesus asks them also to believe in the gospel—to entrust themselves to the word that God has saved his people. They are invited to recognise their salvation *and then* walk in salvation's way.

The call to repentance therefore is at root a call to acknowledge the presence of God's love and its power. To see it merely as a summons to moral rectitude is to impoverish it. What is announced first is that God loves us, and in the very announcement we are asked to return that love. If we want to return it we are thereby committed to love of the neighbour. In the gospel accounts, as a glance will show, Jesus repeatedly reiterates the love-commandment and places it at the heart of the religious and moral response which he asks of his disciples.[21] It is, however, important to remember that Jesus was not primarily a moral teacher. True, as we have seen, what he taught had a bearing on morality. And he did sometimes teach morality directly: the primacy of the love-commandment, the scope and quality of the love which it enjoins, something of what it precludes as well as what it asks to be done. But as with the call to repentance his moral teaching is consequent upon his gospel. It opens up the path of love for one in whom God's love has resonated.

Gospel and Law

The first hearers grasped this well, and it is reflected in the way they shaped their own teaching. First they announced the good news, as had Jesus in announcing the coming of the kingdom; then they explained what this meant in terms of the expectations and preoccupations of Jew or Gentile as the context called for; and then they bade the new disciples to 'let your manner of life be worthy of the gospel of Christ'.[22] Sometimes too they gave specific indications of the kind of behaviour which this required.[23] But always the moral instruction was subordinate to the announcement of the gospel.

Biblical scholarship furnishes a terminology for analysing the foregoing approach. The statement of the essence of the good news is called *kerygma,* a word which means the message of a herald and so is suitable in reference to the *euangelion.* Jesus' own *kerygma,* as we have seen, was characteristically expressed in terms of the coming of God's reign, explicitly or implicitly identified with his own presence. That formula or some version of it featured too in the spreading of the good news by the disciples, and as we saw in Peter's speech to Cornelius its link with Jesus was made by a recital of the main events of his life, with special emphasis on the death and resurrection. What the first preachers were intent above all to convey was that Jesus is the Christ the Son of God, so that their hearers, believing, might have life in his name.[24]

But the preaching of the *kerygma* inevitably gave rise to a need for explanation, called by the scholars *catechesis;* and this assumed a typical shape at an early stage.[25] Our interest is in its ethical component, usually called *didache,* a word which meant teaching—in this context moral instruction. Another biblical term for it is *paraenesis,* meaning, literally, moral exhortation.

I have stressed that in Jesus' teaching moral instruction must be seen in the context of his proclamation of God's reign. The same point is made in the way in which in the gospels' moral teaching is set within a narrative which presents Jesus as inaugurating that reign. But the subordination of moral instruction to religious message is perhaps most clearly seen in the structure of the Pauline and other New Testament letters. The letter to the Romans will serve as an example.

The letter to the Romans is 'the record of the maturing thoughts of Paul, written on the occasion of his impending visit to Rome, in which he formulated the more universal implications of the gospel that he had been preaching'.[26] Paul first considers the way in which God through Christ 'justifies' the person of faith. He goes on to show how God's love assures salvation to all thus justified, paying special attention to the threefold liberation which life 'in Christ' brings: freedom from sin and death, freedom from self through union with Christ, and freedom from the Law. The role of the Spirit in this new life is explored, and the Christian's destiny in 'glory'. The reflections conclude with a paean: 'O the depth of the riches and wisdom and knowledge of God! How unsearchable his judgments and how inscrutable his ways! . . . For from him and through him and to him are all things. To him be glory for ever. Amen.'[27] Only then does Paul turn to moral exhortation.

I chose the letter to the Romans to illustrate the structure of which we have been speaking, the pattern which makes moral *didache* subordinate to the affirmations of the *kerygma,* for in that letter the pattern is seen at its plainest. But the structure may be detected in the other letters too, as theological reflection, often in a mood of thanksgiving or of celebration, leads on to exhortation about good living. We must now look at the exhortation's content.

According to C.H. Dodd the soundest method of determining the contents of the early Christian pattern of teaching is to examine the ethical portions of a number of epistles, and see whether the material common to them all shows any sign of originating at a stage antedating the particular piece. Dodd's own analysis leads to the conclusion that the ethical portions of the epistles are based upon an accepted pattern of teaching which in fact goes back to a very early period, and he considers that the form and content of this teaching can be determined with considerable probability. We can do no better here than reproduce this great scholar's account.

> The convert is first enjoined to lay aside certain discreditable kinds of conduct, especially some which were common and easily condoned in pagan society. Sometimes lists of such vices are inserted, lists which can be shown to have been drawn from popular ethical teaching of the period, quite outside Christianity. The convert is enjoined to abandon these vices and to be prepared for a total reorientation of moral

standards in a Christian sense. This is sometimes expressed in the terms 'to put off the old man and to put on the new'.

Next, some of the typical virtues of the new way of life are set forth, with special emphasis upon such virtues as purity and sobriety, gentleness and humility, generosity and a hospitable temper, patience under injuries, and readiness to forgive.

Then various social relationships are reviewed, in particular those which constitute the family as the primary form of community; the relations of husband and wife, parents and children, master and servants—for, in the social structure of the time, a servant, even if he were a slave, was a member of the *familia*. The proper christian attitude in all such relations is briefly indicated: husbands are to love their wives, children to obey their parents, masters to treat their servants with consideration, and so forth.

Then the wider 'family' of the Christian community itself comes into view. The new member is enjoined to respect the leaders or elders of the society and is taught that each member has his own special function in the body, for which he is responsible.

Looking farther afield, he is given some counsel about behaviour to his pagan neighbours in the delicate situation in which the members of an unpopular sect were likely to find themselves. He must be prudent, nonprovocative, seeking peace, never flouting the social or moral standards of those among whom he lives, while using any opportunity of doing a kindness to them even if they had not been friendly to him.

Like other subjects of the Empire, he is told, he owes obedience to the constituted authorities and should make it a matter of conscience to keep the law and pay his taxes. But there are limits beyond which a higher allegiance claims him: he must be loyal at all cost to his faith, and prepared to endure persecution with inflexible determination and fortitude.

Finally he is reminded of the extremely critical time in which he lives, which calls for constant watchfulness and lays upon him the most solemn responsibilities.[28]

What we need to notice at this point is the *character* of the ethic associated with the preaching of the gospel. It is at once plain that the 'change of heart' was meant to affect day-to-day living and to permeate it through and through. The ambit of that living was manifold: the family and other domestic relations, the larger community of Christians, pagan neighbours, the civil authority. No part of life is untouched by the new experience of faith in Jesus Christ, and all of living is somehow judged by it.

The writings show that the new experience suffused the view of life of the first hearers, and the developing Christian imagination sought ways in which to express the sense of newness engendered by the gospel. And so the early writers spoke of dying and rising with Christ, a second birth, adoption into the family of God's children, putting on the new man. 'The radicality of the metaphors bespeaks a real experience of sharp displacement which many of the converts must have felt.'[29] The first Christians are no longer at ease here, like Eliot's magi after the birth.[30]

And yet there is an ordinariness about the imperatives of the earliest instruction, a kind of modesty which keeps it earthbound. The vices condemned are those which any sound ethic might condemn, the virtues by and large are of a kind aspired to by anyone wishing to live humanely. Christians are not to be conformed to this world, Paul wrote; yet, as one commentator has put it, 'his typical admonitions, which follow those words, are sprinkled with topics and turns of phrase that would be instantly recognisable in the moral rhetoric of his time and place'.[31] Scholars have long acknowledged, as Dodd does in the passage above, that the early writers made use of existing ethical writing in setting out the demands of the Christian way of life.

For of course the early Christian writers were able to draw on a wealth of ethical wisdom from more than one tradition. There was in the first place the Jewish tradition, which formed Jesus himself, and was the background to the first post-pentecost spreading of the gospel in the Jewish homeland and the diaspora. Then there was the moral content of the Graeco-Roman heritage, a natural resource for those who like Paul took the message to the chief cities of the empire. Not that the Christian way was simply identical with that of Israel: and before long that point was tested in the controversy over circumcising gentile converts. Nor that, for example, the detachment from the world prized by the Christians was in the same spirit as that espoused by some stoic philosophers. Yet it was from the moral perceptions of Israel and of Athens and Rome that the early Christians fashioned their 'way'.

Wayne Meeks has expressed the foregoing in these words: 'The meaningful world in which those earliest Christians lived—the world which lived in their heads as well as that which was all around them—was a Jewish world. But the Jewish world was part of the Graeco-Roman world. If therefore we are looking for some "pure" Christian values and beliefs unmixed with the surrounding culture, we are on a fool's errand. What was Christian about the ethos and ethics of those early Christian communities we will discover not by abstraction but by confronting their involvement in the culture of their time and place and seeking to trace the new patterns they made of old forms, to hear the new songs they composed from old melodies.'[32]

Meeks' words serve to warn against the danger of imposing an alien schema upon a process so complex as is here described. Yet it happens that a modern theological debate offers one way of coping with a key issue, as for our purposes, however summarily, we must. The debate concerns the precise character or as it is sometimes called the identity of Christian morality. In view of the account of morality with which this book opened, the way in which the question arises might be put as follows: if morality is a matter of general human experience and if its prescriptions are accessible to reason, what role does Christian faith play? The question is often put in the form, is there a specifically Christian morality?

What Was New?

Here we can only try to simplify a complex and continuing debate; and this account is based in the main upon the Roman Catholic experience of the question. In that experience the debate began when moral theologians, critical of accounts of Christian ethics which scarcely referred to Christ or Christian sources, called for a return to the Bible as the source-book of all Christian theologising. There ensued a recovery of focus on the person and teaching of Jesus Christ; and his emphasis upon the love-commandment was taken to be the essential mark of any account of morality which wished to be Christian.

But what *was* this love? It was soon seen that to give concrete content to the love-commandment one needed to have recourse to specific prescriptions such as those of the Decalogue and of the ethical teaching of the gospels and other New Testament books. And so love of the neighbour was seen to be expressed in concrete norms: negative, as in prohibitions on killing, say, or stealing or lying; positive in injunctions to be just or peaceful or truthful, or whatever the particular virtue or action.

But then a new kind of question suggested itself. Are not these precepts of peace and justice and respect for life and truthfulness, whether positively or negatively expressed, what anyone who thought about the prerequisites of a good life would see as necessary? The emergence of this type of question was influenced by two quite diverse (though of course sometimes overlapping) developments.

One was the work of scripture scholars who were finding parallels between the moral teaching of the Scriptures and that from other religious and even secular sources. It was noted for example that the main provisions of the Decalogue were the same, if differently formulated, as those of the Babylonian Code of Hammurabi. And I have already alluded to Paul's use of the stoic lists of virtues and vices, and mentioned the secular origins of other parts of the early Christian ethic. Such scholarly findings gave point to the question, is there anything in the moral teaching of the Bible, even of Jesus himself, that is not available to reason reflecting on human experience in the world?

A second stimulus came from quite another direction. It is again somewhat of a simplification but I hope not unfair to say that in the sixties and seventies Anglo-American moral philosophy began to make an impact upon Catholic moral theology for the first time. And one of the ways in which it impinged was in creating an awareness of the ways in which a particular type of moral prescription is inevitably time-bound and culture-bound. Thus was raised a question about the present status of some of the biblical teaching: obvious examples are Paul's injunctions concerning slavery and concerning women. Inevitably it came to be asked, is there anything in the biblical moral teaching which is not in the end to be judged at the bar of reason? Which is another way of asking whether there is anything in the moral teaching of the Bible, even of Jesus himself, that is not available to reason reflecting on human experience in the world.

Two Approaches

The two lines of response which this question has evoked have been called respectively the 'Autonomy' and *Glaubensethik* schools. The former are so called from the apparent autonomy which they attribute to morality vis-à-vis religion—though, as we shall see, the autonomy is relative and not absolute. The latter school gets its name from the German word for faith, and the name implies a view of morality which connects it closely with religious belief. One of the ways in which the issue between them is often formulated is whether or to what extent 'revelation' is necessary to morality.

In answering this question writers of the Autonomy school are in general reluctant to grant that the revelation made in Jesus Christ has contributed anything to our knowledge of morality's *content*. Another way of putting this is to say that one does not need Christian faith to know what morality requires. These writers concede that revelation and faith give a *context* to moral striving, as the Covenant gave a context to the Israelites' keeping the Torah. Many of them grant that a Christian vision gives additional *motivation* for right behaviour: we love the neighbour for him/herself, but also as brother or sister in the Lord. And of course the Christian has, in the person of Jesus, a *model* and an *inspiration* for moral endeavour. But what to do or refrain from doing, in the cause of justice or peace or any other moral value, is in its substance the same.

Writers in the *Glaubensethik* school agree with the autonomists concerning context and motivation and the exemplary significance of Jesus. Where they disagree is upon the question of content, for they maintain that in the Christian moral way there are requirements whose existence and character and binding force are known only because of revelation. Of course the substance of morality's claims are accessible to reason, they say, and so shared by all people of good will. But in the *Glaubensethik* view it is nevertheless the case that there are things asked of Christians which are recognised only in faith.

One might think that this must be an issue of fact which could be settled by recourse to the sources of the revelation. One might expect, that is, that the *Glaubensethik* authors could provide a list of moral demands which are known only from Scripture and/or from the tradition of the Church, and which cannot be perceived as obligatory by the use of reason alone. If they can do this, one might think, their position is vindicated; if not, the autonomists have it.

The matter, however, is not so simple. The authors of the *Glaubensethik* do indeed provide a list (or lists, for they differ a little as between themselves).[33] But the autonomists respond by contending that some of the items on the list are instances of religious rather than moral obligation, while others are taught in the Catholic tradition as grounded in reason as much as they are in faith.

In order to decide between the two positions we should have to agree in the first place upon the respective scopes of religion and morality and to consider the import of the tradition's grounding of positions in faith as well as in reason. We should also, as Vincent MacNamara has done, analyse each side's use of such terms as 'content' and 'motivation'.[34] But this task is too vast in the present context so for the sake of later argument I shall sketch summarily a working position.

The Makings of a Response

We might begin by recalling the incontrovertible. It is incontrovertible that the Judaeo-Christian theological inheritance provides a context in which the moral pilgrimage of humanity may be seen in a way which enhances it. There is the doctrine of creation, with its view of humans as made in the image of God and so called to take part in the very making of the world. There is the theme of human stewardship of creation, suggestive of an accountability for what is in our power and charge. Then there is the doctrine of sin, the 'sin of the world' and personal sin, a dark shadow on the *imago dei* which threatens death to the human spirit. And of course there is salvation: the news of a gracious God who has not left us in the prison of our sin but in Christ has freed us to 'return'.

It is incontrovertible too that in the moral teaching of Jesus the love-commandment is primary: all the Law and the Prophets are summarised in it. And in the teaching of Jesus we find abundant illustration of the quality of the love which is called for. It is in the first place a matter of the 'heart' (a Hebrew metaphor for the core of the personality) but it is expressed in action which is provident and caring. It is universal in its scope: the disciple is asked to love even the enemy. It is compassionate and forgiving and persists even in the face of rejection. It is radical and boundlessly generous. It is like God's love; indeed it *is* God's love, for we are capable of it only because God first loved us.

It can perhaps be said that the love thus characterised exceeds the 'merely rational', if rational in this context bespeaks something which may be concluded as a result of reason's reflection on human nature. And it makes demands which appear to transcend what might 'reasonably' be expected: one of its distinctive features, for example, is an unlimited readiness to forgive even those who have done us great wrong. *Agape,* to use the New Testament's word for this kind of loving, is more than urbanity.

It may be said also, on the evidence of the biblical material, that the translation of this love into action displays some characteristic emphases. There is the readiness to forgive just mentioned; there is also a concern with 'justice', and a special concern for the widow and the orphan— Hebrew metaphors for the specially needy. There is the message of the parable that unless the grain of wheat dies it does not bring forth fruit.

But it will no doubt be noticed that all of these features—unlimited readiness to forgive, a preoccupation with justice, a bias towards the specially vulnerable, an openness to the 'cross'—are in the first place matters of quality and emphasis and orientation. They indicate the *character* of the love to which a disciple is called: the readiness to forgive is 'unlimited', concern with justice is a 'preoccupation', service of the poor is by way of 'bias', crucifixion for most is metaphorical. These pointers to the way of the Christian disciple do not on their face say anything about the *content* of concrete actions.

Not that the Bible lacks concrete precepts: that is, precepts which name acts or attitudes or states of affairs or omissions enjoined on us or prohibited by *agape*. 'Thou shalt not kill', for example, is a plain state-ment of the kind of action excluded under the new as under the old covenant. 'Love is patient and kind', says Paul; 'love is not jealous or boastful; it is not arrogant or rude.'[35] 'It has been reported to me by Chloe's people that there is quarrelling among you', he writes reprovingly to the Corinthians.[36] 'I was hungry and you gave me no food', the King will say to those on his left hand; 'I was thirsty and you gave me no drink, I was a stranger and you did not welcome me, naked and you did not clothe me, sick and in prison and you did not visit me.'[37]

But the precepts of the 'second table' of the Decalogue—those which concern our innerworldy relationships—and the concrete norms of the earliest Christian teaching are found also outside of the biblical books, for they belong too to the currency of other ethical traditions. We might say that they are the kind of imperative which any well-meaning, right-thinking person might recognise. Reverting to an earlier perspective, we might say that we do not need revelation or faith to know of them or to see how they could oblige us. And of course the concrete norms of biblical times must be interpreted with care, for they were forged in the life of a distant time and place. Paul's injunctions to slaves have outgrown their usefulness, as has certain of his teaching about the relationship of husband and wife. The Bible says nothing concrete about nuclear weapons or computer ethics or test-tube babies or public education programmes on AIDS.

So even if it be agreed (and agreement, as already said, would presuppose a considerable clarification of terms) that there is some revealed content at the core of the Chrisian moral scheme, we are not relieved from thinking through the practical demands of morality as these disclose themselves in each age. Our path will be illuminated by the great Christian affirmations about the world and about humanity, our thinking shaped by what has been handed on to us out of generations of experience of life in the Spirit of Christ. But in this as in other dimensions of the human task grace builds on nature, and there is no shortcut to moral wisdom or achievement.

We turn next to an aspect of early Christian experience which has a more particular bearing on our theme: the Christian community's relationship with outsiders and especially with the civil authority. Earlier we glimpsed an unease felt by converts in the religious and secular environments in which they found themselves. Their sense of urgency in regard to spreading the gospel was considerable and it was reinforced, it seems, by a belief that the form of this world was in any case passing away. But we have seen also that the typical *didache* included some instruction upon their relationship with neighbours who were not of the faith, and that its tone was moderate and forbearing. We shall see now that there emerged also a gradual recognition of the need to make terms with the requirements of life in the *polis*.

Churches and Synagogues

The first neighbours were Jewish, and the converts' relationships with them were bound to be sensitive: think of how we can feel when a family member or friend changes religious allegiance. At first the members of the new community continued to live outwardly in the ordinary Jewish way. As Rudolf Schnackenburg has remarked: 'How else would it have been possible for their people not to look upon them as a disloyal separate community, but to look on them with benevolence (cf. Acts 2:47) and for many, including even priests(6:7) and Pharisees(15:5) to join them?'[38] But in time it was necessary to insist upon a radical theological difference between the ancient tradition and the new way, as the Christians were forced to an explicit rejection of the belief that salvation came through observance of the Law.

The way in which this came into prominence is told in the Acts of the Apostles. 'Now the apostles and the brethren who were in Judaea heard that the Gentiles also had received the word of God. So when Peter went up to Jerusalem, the circumcision party criticised him, saying "Why did you go to uncircumcised men and eat with them?" '[39] The circumcision party were those who contended that converts had to observe everything which the old law prescribed. This particular complaint can be looked at both as objecting to the violation of a traditional dietary law and as requiring circumcision for entry into what would soon be called the Christian community. Peter's reply is to recount the vision which had brought him to see that salvation was for the gentiles too. The vision included a repudiation of another dietary regulation—that which pronounced certain foods unclean—and led Peter's hearers to acknowledge that 'to the Gentiles also God has granted repentance unto life'.[40]

But the dispute did not end there, and chapter fifteen opens with the information that some men came down from Judaea and were teaching the brethren, 'Unless you were circumcised according to the custom of Moses, you cannot be saved.'[41] The result was what became known as the Council of Jerusalem, at which after 'much debate' Peter reiterated the freedom of the gentiles from merely ceremonial or cultic traditional observance.[42] The question of eating with gentiles itself was to surface again, as it came to be asked whether Jewish Christians living according to the Mosaic law should share a common table with gentile

Christians. And Paul tells the Galatians how he stood up to Peter who for fear of the circumcision party had begun to vacillate. Paul's own position was uncompromising: 'I said to Cephas before them all, "If you, though a Jew, live like a Gentile and not like a Jew, how can you compel the Gentiles to live like Jews?" '[43]

Yet the stance *vis-à-vis* the Jewish environment was respectful, and neither Paul nor the others denied the right of Jewish Christians to live after the Jewish manner.[44] Paul shows a like sensitivity in a well-known passage in the letter to the Romans. Of this Schnackenburg has written: 'Probably we should identify the "weak" in Rome (Rom. 14:1-15:3) mainly with former Jews who could still not accustom themselves no longer to observe certain days (14:5) and the distinction between clean and unclean foods (14:14,20). Paul was even ready to show them consideration.'[45]

The early letters gave instruction too on the behaviour of the Christians toward their pagan neighbours. On matters of principle there was to be no compromise: they were not, for example, to take part in pagan sacrifice, for 'what pagans sacrifice they offer to demons and not to God'.[46] But a sectarian fanaticism is inappropriate. So the Corinthians should 'eat whatever is sold in the meat market without raising any question on the ground of conscience'.[47] Moreover, 'if one of the unbelievers invites you to dinner and you are disposed to go, eat whatever is set before you without raising any question on the ground of conscience'.[48] Both these injunctions refer to the possibility of the Christian's being offered, at the market or as dinner guests, food which has been sacrificed to idols. The Christian is not to make unnecessary fuss. Yet if acceptance is accorded a potentially scandalous significance ('If someone says to you "This has been offered in sacrifice" '), then 'out of consideration for the man who informed you, and for conscience' sake—I mean his conscience, not yours—do not eat it'.[49]

Caesar's Coin

More precisely to the point of our concern is the attitude of the new community toward the civil authority and its institutions. Mark records this as having come in question explicitly during the mission of Jesus himself.[50] Jesus' activities had aroused the anger of the chief priests and scribes and elders, and they sent some Pharisees and Herodians 'to entrap him in his talk'. The subject of their intervention was a census tax which the Romans had levied upon the inhabitants of Judea, Samaria and Idumea. The tax was controversial among the Jews for in addition to being a permanent reminder of their subjection to Rome it provoked religious scruples. This was because it had to be paid in coins bearing the Emperor's image, whereas the Jews acknowledged only God or his representative as sovereign. The question 'is it lawful to pay taxes to Caesar, or not?' was intended to discredit Jesus among both nationalistic Jews and those who favoured the link with Rome.[51]

A full account of the meaning of Jesus' reply—'Render to Caesar the things that are Caesar's, and to God the things are God's'[52]—is beyond our present purpose. It will be enough to observe that Mark took Jesus' pronouncement as an endorsement of the principle that loyalty to the civil authority need not contradict obedience to God.[53] The point is made by Schnackenburg thus: 'Emperor and God, State and divine rule are for Jesus two realities, belonging to two different orders, though not juxtaposed unrelatedly, and there is no question which of the two for him is the higher, incomparably higher. He leaves the secular and at that time the pagan State its rights in its own sphere, but only to the extent that the all-embracing rights of God over man are not thereby violated.'[54]

Schnackenburg elsewhere remarks that though Jesus' reply showed the early Church the line it should take in its attitude to the public authorities, 'that terse saying did not relieve it of the task of determining its actual relationship with those in authority'.[55] Something of what the emergent community made of that relationship may be gleaned from a reading of other New Testament writings.

Of course we need not expect to find a full-blown doctrine of Church-State relations. For one thing it took time for the little communities of Christians to develop sufficiently defined mutual bonds to generate a sense of 'Church,' as distinct from 'Churches'. And issues of relationship with civil society arose only piecemeal and incidentally. Alec Vidler has described the general situation: 'After Pentecost, the church of Christ soon became a distinct society, but in the New Testament period it was never more than a small minority within the Roman Empire. All it looked for, so far as civil government was concerned, was freedom and security for its missionary work. There was no question yet of formal relations between civil government and ecclesiastical organisation.'[56]

Christians in the Polis

We have already touched on what Meeks called the sense of displacement which the gospel engendered in the converts. And any sense of estrangement was bound to have made itself felt especially in the domain of their relationship with temporal power and its institutions. Jewish Christians had already had to contend with the fact that the land of a proud people must now count as no more than a province of Rome. And we have seen that the religious claims of the emperor were in direct conflict with the religious role of Jewish civil leadership, as well as with the most basic conviction of the followers of Jesus. Add to this a sense of the imminence of the last times, and an impatience with and detachment from secular institutions must have been inevitable.

Indeed we get a glimpse of this in the early Paul, as when he conveys to the Thessalonians a sense of their apartness: 'But we exhort you, brethren . . . to aspire to live quietly, to mind your own affairs, and to work with your hands, as we charged you; so that you may command the respect of outsiders, and be dependent on nobody.'[57] Later, more pointedly, he reproves the Corinthians for taking their quarrels before the pagan courts.[58] Yet, as we have seen, the Corinthians are not to comport themselves eccentrically in the secular environment. And by the time of writing the letter to the Romans Paul is speaking of the authority of the civil government as being from God.

It is interesting to read this passage in full.

> Let every person be subject to the governing authorities. For there is no authority except from God, and those that exist have been instituted by God. Therefore he who resists the authorities resists what God has appointed, and those who resist will incur judgment. For rulers are not a terror to good conduct, but to bad. Would you have no fear of him who is in authority? Then do what is good, and you will receive his approval, for he is God's servant for your good. But if you do wrong, be afraid, for he does not bear the sword in vain; he is the servant of God, to execute his wrath on the wrongdoer. Therefore one must be subject, not only to avoid God's wrath but also for the sake of conscience. For the same reason you must pay taxes, for the authorities are ministers of God, attending to this very thing. Pay all of them their dues, taxes to whom taxes are due, revenue to whom revenue is due, respect to whom respect is due, honour to whom honour is due.[59]

This has puzzled commentators, partly because it seems a little out of place in the context in which it occurs, in the letter to the Romans, partly because of its apparently unreserved and unexpected regard for the secular authority. Some have thought it an interpolation, but this seems unlikely.[60] For a proper grasp of its import it is necessary to keep some points in mind.

First, it is natural that Paul should have addressed matters of civic duty; these were, after all, an aspect of life in community with others, meant to be regulated by justice and by love. And the Christians of Rome were bound to have been especially conscious of the imperial authorities and institutions. Second, the passage is not at all at odds with the general tenor of Paul's teaching: 'Despite St Paul's not always satisfactory experiences, there is not a word in his writings against the empire.'[61] Third, it assumes throughout that the authorities are 'conducting themselves uprightly and are seeking the interests of the community'.[62] As Fitzmyer writes: 'The possibility is not envisaged either of a tyrannical government or of one failing to cope with a situation where the just rights of individual citizens or of a minority group are neglected.'[63] Fourth, Paul is here concerned solely with the duties of subjects of legitimate authority, and not with duties of its bearers.

The same teaching is found in the first letter of Peter: 'Be subject for the Lord's sake to every human institution, whether it be to the emperor as supreme, or to the governors as sent by him to punish those who do wrong and to praise those who do right. For it is God's will that by doing right you should put to silence the ignorance of foolish men. Live as free men, yet without using your freedom as a pretext for evil; but live as servants of God. Honour all men. Love the brotherhood. Fear God. Honour the emperor.'[64] Similar exhortations are found in the letter to Titus,[65] and in the first letter to Timothy,[66] where prayer for the authorities is called for.

What we see expressed in the data here reviewed therefore is a sense both of apartness and of continuity. The sense of apartness is stronger in the earlier writing, as might be expected, given the belief that the end of the 'present age' was imminent. As the believers came to discover that the parousia was not yet, they settled down to make Christian sense of the secular life around them. This process included a recognition of the role of government and its institutions, and of the fact that membership of a Christian community did not exempt people from the usual civic duties.

Upon one point however the converts were unrepentantly at odds with the ethos in which Christianity was making its way, and that was the religious pretensions of civil rulers. The key text here is the Apocalypse—composed, according to the majority of scholars, during the persecution of Christians which occurred towards the end of the reign of the emperor Domitian (d. AD 96).[67] The gradual apotheosis of the emperor was a product of the religious spirit of the time[68] and was soon seen by the State to be an important instrument in consolidating the unity of the empire. A religion which was both exclusivist and supranational was bound to draw the wrath of the authorities, and from the time of Nero (54-68) Christians began to be persecuted.

A refusal to worship the emperor was probably what immediately occasioned the persecution of Christians under Domitian,[69] and the Apocalypse may be seen as expressing the Christian reaction to this. Schnackenburg comments that it is significant that the Apocalypse ascribes the power of the State which is blasphemously abused, not to God but to Satan. 'The State that deifies itself, the ruler who exceeds his competence and treads the honour of God under his feet, is an instrument of Satan.'[70]

The import of the main material from the New Testament concerning the developing relationships between the new faith and the civic setting in which it was forged has been expressed by Rudolf Schnackenburg in these words: 'The early Christian conception of the state . . . remains unharmonized to a certain extent; but Jesus' exhortation to give to Caesar the things that are Caesar's, and to God the things that are God's lies at the point of intersection of the two lines, one leading to God and the other leading to Satan. Romans 13 and Apocalypse 13 are not two mutually exclusive pictures, but rather the two different sides of one coin . . .'[71]

Our review of the biblical data was meant to achieve two things. First it was intended to give a sense of what the emergent Christian community made of morality. Their gospel was that a new reign of God's love was begun in the work of Jesus Christ; and this had implications for daily living. For love begets love, and the news that God loves is an invitation to love in return. The central Christian commandment was that we are to love both God and the neighbour. Indications of what this meant in practice are in the teaching and example of Jesus; and what it further meant in the concrete was worked out in the unfolding experience of the earliest Christians. The new Church was concerned with right moral living therefore; but its concern was secondary to its witness to the saving love of God.

Among the specific concerns of the early Christians was that of relating to the civil authority; and a sense of what they made of this was the second objective of our review. The Christians' task was complicated by the Roman dimension of political existence in the territories in which the first Churches made their way. It was further complicated by a widespread if temporary belief that the world as they knew it was coming to an end. But what we find on the whole is a readiness to render to Caesar and to God respectively what was seen as belonging to each.

4

THE CHURCH IN THE MODERN WORLD

In the same way as the young Church discovered itself in its interaction with the world of its time so the Church today comes to know itself more fully in relationship with the modern world. The Church is still a community gathered in the faith that Jesus is Lord and by the same token sent to proclaim that Jesus is Lord. But what that means from age to age is progressively disclosed, as the community in fidelity to its tradition engages with the changing times.

The Church's understanding of itself is therefore always in process. But the process is sometimes punctuated by moments of special significance. The Second Vatican Council was such a moment, for in that event the Roman Catholic Church engaged, selfconsciously and deliberately, with the world in which it finds itself now. Some of what the Council made of the encounter is already obsolete, much of it yet to be realised. But the Council's understanding of the Church and of its mission is an indispensable touchstone in the ongoing work of theology.

Institution or Communion?
As is to be expected, the Council's theology of the Church itself is the key to the present self-understanding of the Roman Catholic Church. And a simple way to grasp what that means is to contrast the first draft of its main document about the Church with what was eventually enacted by the Council Fathers. The material of the draft was organised under eleven headings, and even the sequence and the wording are telling.

1. The nature of the Church militant.
2. The members of the Church and the necessity of the Church for salvation.
3. The episcopate as the highest grade of the sacrament of orders; the priesthood.
4. Residential bishops.
5. The states of evangelical perfection.
6. The laity.

7. The teaching office (magisterium) of the Church.
8. Authority and obedience in the Church.
9. Relationships between the Church and State and religious tolerance.
10. The necessity of proclaiming the gospel to all peoples and in the whole world.
11. Ecumenism.

An appendix dealt with the 'Virgin Mary, Mother of God and Mother of Men'.[1]

Plainly, institutional themes predominated: that is, those aspects of the Church which have to do with its organisation as a visible society in the world. And the institution is conceived upon a markedly hierarchical model, the familiar 'pyramid' whose apex is the pope and base the laity, with the bishops, priests and religious in between. There is no lack of confidence in the terms in which the institution presents itself and its purposes.

The Council's critique of the draft was vigorous. The best-known intervention is probably that of Bishop de Smedt of Bruges whose criticism has been summarised by a commentator as follows: 'when the Church describes its mission, it must avoid "triumphalism"; it must not, therefore, present itself as though it were bent on conquest, and as though it strode from victory to victory; it must not reduce its own life to the activity of the hierarchy and so allow itself to be fascinated by "clericalism"; finally, it must make no concessions to "juridicalism".'[2]

A speech by Bishop Elchinger of Strasbourg incorporated both a critique of the document and a sketch of what was needed in its stead. 'Yesterday . . . the church was considered above all as an institution, today it is experienced as a community. Yesterday it was the pope who was mainly in view, today the pope is thought of as united with the bishops. Yesterday the bishop alone was considered, today all the bishops together. Yesterday theology stressed the importance of the hierarchy, today it is discovering the importance of the people of God. Yesterday it was chiefly concerned with what divided, today it voices all that unites. Yesterday the theology of the Church was mainly preoccupied with the inward life of the Church, today it sees the Church as orientated to the outside world.'[3]

The Constitution *Lumen Gentium* reflects the impact of these and like comments, as the sequence and wording of its chapter headings in turn suggest.

1. The Mystery of the Church
2. The People of God
3. The Church is Hierarchical

4. The Laity
5. The Call to Holiness
6. Religious
7. The Pilgrim Church
8. Our Lady

It is easy to see that the institutional aspect is here no longer dominant. The Church now is in the first place 'mystery': a 'reality imbued with the hidden presence of God', as Paul VI explained in opening the Council's second session. It is also a 'people', a community whose ultimate historic roots are in God's choice of Israel; now, after Christ, a people of the New Covenant, making its way in history toward history's end. There is an institutional dimension, but the institutional elements obtain their significance through their service of the other dimensions. There is still a hierarchical ministry, but its place is in the mediation of the mystery and the building up of the communion.

A Church in the World

Lumen Gentium embodies the Council's reflection upon the inner nature of the Church. The concerns of the document are in the main domestic, its idiom that of the world of theology. But the Council was not content with a domestic reflection, and it wished also to address the world outside the Catholic Church's visible boundaries. Hence its 'pastoral Constitution' on the Church in the modern world, called *Gaudium et Spes* from the opening words of its opening paragraph. That paragraph and the paragraph which follows it give a sense of the Constitution's mood and intent.

> The joy and hope, the grief and anguish of the people of our time, especially of those who are poor or afflicted in any way, are the joy and hope, the grief and anguish of the followers of Christ as well. Nothing that is genuinely human fails to find an echo in their hearts. For theirs is a community composed of people who, united in Christ and guided by the Holy Spirit, press onwards towards the kingdom of the Father and are bearers of the message of salvation intended for all. That is why Christians cherish a feeling of deep solidarity with the human race and its history.[4]
>
> Now that the Second Vatican Council has deeply studied the mystery of the Church, it resolutely addresses not only the children of the Church and all who call upon the name of Christ, but the whole of humanity as well, and it longs to set forth the way it understands the presence and functions of the Church in the world of today.[5]

Later we shall be attempting to develop an account of the Church and its relationship with the world. But it will help now if we attend to some themes of the Council which are of particular importance in this enterprise. The first is its bringing into prominence of the laity.

Lay People in the Church

Writing in 1953 Yves Congar, whose own work had considerable influence in the process, describes the re-discovery of the role of the lay member of the Church. 'First of all there were the great nineteenth-century leaders, with the first ideas of what was to become Catholic Action. Nearer our own time there was the double movement, liturgical and apostolic or missionary, which is still expanding in all directions. With a return to liturgical sources people here and there began more and more to realise that the laity is indeed that *plebs sancta*, that consecrated people, of which the canon of the Mass speaks, and that this people has an active part in public worship, the central act of the Church's life. It is in the liturgical movement that we first find a renewed consciousness of the mystery of the Church and of the ecclesial character of the laity. There followed a renewing of the theology and spirituality of marriage . . . In the field of apostolic expansion of the Church, the faithful were at the same time redis-covering both the great dignity and the great demands of the Christian obligation.'[6]

The very terminology used in this description situates it in pre-conciliar times.[7] But some of the factors listed by Congar may come as a surprise: 'the renewed interest in mysticism, the demand for religious books, the importance given to holiness lived in the world, the return to the Bible; and, as regards the clergy, the momentous beginning of a change in the matter of clericalism and clerical attitudes'.[8] It will of course be remembered that Congar was writing in the context of a mainland western European experience.

At any rate it is plain that there was by then in train a series of developments which found an apt outlet in the Council. A comprehensive statement of that assembly's articulation of a theology of the laity would require that we attend to virtually every Council document, for there is scarcely a theme of the Council that does not bear upon those develop-ments. But we shall have to be content with synopsis, and a passage from the Decree on the Apostolate of Lay People will serve us well.

> In the Church there is diversity of ministry but unity of mission. To the apostles and their successors Christ has entrusted the office of teaching, sanctifying and governing in his name and by his power. But the laity are made to share in the priestly, prophetical and kingly office of Christ; they

have therefore, in the Church and in the world, their own assignment in
the mission of the whole People of God. In the concrete, their apostolate
is exercised when they work at the evangelization and sanctification of
people; it is exercised too when they endeavour to have the Gospel spirit
permeate and improve the temporal order, going about it in a way that
bears witness to Christ and helps forward the salvation of humanity. The
characteristic of the lay state being a life led in the midst of the world and
of secular affairs, lay people are called by God to make of their apostolate,
through the vigor of their Christian spirit, a leaven in the world.[9]

Here is a call to lay members of the Church to assume a responsibility
for the spread of the gospel. And it is not as though they are merely
mandated by the hierarchy to assist them in the work of the gospel. For
they themselves possess a share in the triple office of Christ; and so they
have 'their own' assignment in the mission of the 'People of God'. They
fulfil this assignment not merely 'when they work at the evangelisation
and sanctification of people', but also inasmuch as they 'endeavour to
have the gospel spirit permeate and improve the temporal order'.

This mission is carried out in the first place in the concrete
circumstances of each person's life—at home, at work, in the family, in
wider social relationships—according to the unique vocation of each.
It is accomplished when a man loves his wife, a child her parent; when
a worker is given a fair wage and gives a fair return; when truth is told
and promises kept. Wherever love is, there is God, said St Augustine;
and where love is lived there is witness to the gospel of grace.

The Autonomy of the Secular
Related to the theme of lay responsibility for the gospel is an
acknowledgment that 'it is to the laity, though not exclusively to them,
that secular duties and activity properly belong'.[10]

> Let them be aware of what their faith demands of them in these matters
> and derive strength from it; . . . It is their task to cultivate a properly
> informed conscience and to impress the divine law on the affairs of the
> earthly city. For guidance and spiritual strength let them turn to the
> clergy; but let them realise that their pastors will not always be so expert
> as to have a ready answer to every problem (even every grave problem)
> that arises; that is not the role of the clergy; it is rather up to lay people
> to shoulder their responsibilities under the guidance of Christian wisdom
> and with eager attention to the teaching authority of the Church.[11]

In the preceding paragraph the Council made it plain that 'Christ
did not bequeath to the Church a mission in the political, economic,
or social order: the purpose he assigned to it was a religious one.'[12]

Granted, the Church's religious message has an important bearing upon life in the world, but it does not furnish concrete answers to questions which come within the purview of such secular disciplines as economics or politics. Indeed more than one concrete solution may be reconcilable with the Gospel message ; whereas often 'Christian vision will suggest a certain solution in some given situation', it nevertheless happens 'rather frequently, and legitimately so, that some of the faithful, with no less sincerity, will see the problem quite differently.'[13] In that case, care should be taken not to lend the authority of the Church to what is open to difference of opinion.

What we have in these passages is an emphasis on specifically lay competence and responsibility, and an intimation of an autonomy of the secular. The character of this autonomy and the validity of its claim has already been explained in the document: 'If by the autonomy of earthly affairs is meant the gradual discovery, exploitation, and ordering of the laws and values of matter and society, then the demand for autonomy is perfectly in order; it is at once the claim of modern man and the desire of the creator.'[14] The context makes it clear that the Council here has in mind the autonomy of the sciences especially, but it is plain that the principle extends to secular pursuits in general. There is, it need hardly be said, no suggestion that this autonomy amounts to an independence of the moral order.

'Open to the World'

Another theme of *Gaudium et Spes* is of interest to us: what is sometimes called its 'openness to the world'. The sense of 'world' which is most obviously in question here is that part of the human community which is not 'church'. The note is struck as early as the opening paragraphs already quoted, and is sustained throughout the document, sometimes incidentally, sometimes more formally and explicitly.

So for example in a discussion of conscience there is the remark that 'through loyalty to conscience, Christians are joined to others in the search for truth and for the right solution to so many moral problems which arise both in the life of individuals and from social relationships'.[15] Later we are told, 'Those also have a claim on our respect and charity who think and act differently from us in social, political, and religious matters.'[16] This point is in due course amplified, in the Council's statements on relations with other Churches and also in its Declaration on Religious Freedom.

An aspect of the Council's openness to the world is its refusal to see a dichotomy between spiritual and temporal aspects of its task or to conceive its mission in other-worldly terms. True, 'it has a saving and eschatological purpose which can be fully attained only in the next life'.[17] But it is now here present on earth, and composed of people who, 'members of the earthly city, are called to form the family of the children of God even in this present century of mankind and to increase it continually until the Lord comes'.[18] The Church is at once a visible organisation and a spiritual community, and it 'travels the same journey of all mankind and shares the same earthly lot with the world'.[19] In this journey it both gives and receives: it believes that it can contribute much to humanising the family of man;[20] but it also gladly values what other Churches and even secular experience contribute in the achievement of this aim.[21]

A Pilgrim Church

Mention of the human journey recalls a last theme of the Council which we must notice: the theme of the pilgrim Church. Chapter Seven of *Lumen Gentium* begins: 'The Church, to which we are all called in Christ Jesus, and in which by the grace of God we acquire holiness, will receive its perfection only in the glory of heaven, when will come the time of the renewal of all things (Acts 3:21). At the same time, together with the human race, the universe itself, which is so closely related to man and which attains its destiny through him, will be perfectly reestablished in Christ (cf. Eph.1:10; Col.1:20; 2Pet.3:10-13)'.[22]

In question here is what is called in theology the eschatological dimension of the message of salvation. The word eschatology comes from a Greek expression meaning 'the last things', and in Christian theology it refers to doctrines or beliefs concerning the end of this life, considered from the standpoint either of the individual or of the race. Under the rubric of eschatology, classical tracts treated death, judgment, heaven, hell and purgatory. Underlying these themes is a general belief concerning the provisional character of human history: that the form of this world is passing away and that we have not here a lasting city.[23]

What this means for the Church is explained by the Council:

> Already the final age of the world is with us and the renewal of the world is irrevocably under way; it is even now anticipated in a certain real way, for the Church on earth is endowed already with a sanctity which is real though imperfect. However, until there be realized new heavens and a new earth where justice dwells the pilgrim Church, in its sacraments and institutions, which belong to the present age, carries the mark of this world which will pass, and she herself takes her place among the creatures which groan and travail yet and await the revelation of the sons of God.[24]

The Church is holy, but not wholly so; its earthly form anticipates the eschaton but not completely. It is called to eternal glory but its temporal manifestation is imperfect and provisional. It is the bearer of a salvation which is always in the making until Christ will come again.

We have been reviewing some themes of the Second Vatican Council which have a special bearing on the concerns of this book. We saw that the Council quite purposely ended the dominance of an institutional model of Church, replacing it with a conception which expressed mystical and communitarian dimensions. Ministry was to be seen as service, of the mystery and of the community; and the vocation of each member (and not just of the hierarchy) in living the gospel and in spreading it was underlined. The emphasis on lay responsibility was matched by a recognition of lay competence, and a 'rightful autonomy' in secular affairs was acknowledged. And the Church was conceived as 'open to the world', and in sympathy with the moral and spiritual striving of all people of good will. It is also a pilgrim Church, not yet in full possession of the holiness to which it is called.

Models of the Church?

An adequate understanding of the Church in the modern world must incorporate these perspectives and emphases. Here we can only hint at the lines of such an understanding, and we shall do so with the aid of a valuable analysis made by Avery Dulles.[25]

Dulles borrowed the concept of 'model' from the methodology of the physical and social sciences, and we may spare ourselves a technical digression if we think of it simply as a particularly suggestive kind of analogy. In our context it is a way of looking at the Church which is more or less fruitful in insight into the Church's nature. Dulles describes five such ways and what they disclose about the Church, noting their respective disadvantages as well as their merits.

Two of the five models concern mainly the Church 'in itself', so to speak. The first of these is the institutional model, according to which the Church is seen as a society which, in words of B.C. Butler quoted by Dulles, has 'a constitution, a set of rules, a governing body, and a set of actual members who accept this constitution and these rules as binding on them'.[26] Here the emphasis is upon the external visible features of the Church.

The second model views the Church as a communion, 'at once inward and external, an inner communion of spiritual life (of faith, hope and charity) signified and engendered by an external communion in profession of the faith, discipline and the sacramental life'.[27] Two images are especially congenial to this model, the mystical body of Christ and the people of God, for in each is combined both spiritual and visible aspects.

The three other models which Dulles examines are the Church as Sacrament, as Herald and as Servant. Each of these contains a stronger and more explicit external reference. As sacrament the Church is a sign to the world, and it is the instrument of what it signifies; as herald it preaches the gospel in the world; and as servant it ministers to the world's search for truth and goodness. To the extent that they make this external reference explicit these models are perhaps more apt than the first two in terms of our objectives here.

Of course, as Avery Dulles is at pains to stress, what the models offer are complementary ways of looking at the Church. 'Each model of the Church has its weaknesses; no one should be canonized as the measure of all the rest. Instead of searching for some absolutely best image, it would be advisable to recognize that the manifold images given to us by Scripture and Tradition are mutually complementary. They should be made to interpenetrate and mutually qualify one another. None, therefore, should be interpreted in an exclusivistic sense, so as to negate what the other approved models have to teach us'.[28]

Yet one need not view them as equally valuable in disclosing the nature of the Church. Dulles himself is emphatic upon one point in particular: 'One of the five models, I believe, cannot properly be taken as primary— and this is the institutional model. Of their very nature, I believe, institutions are subordinate to persons, structures are subordinate to life . . . Without calling into question the value and importance of institutions, one may feel that this value does not properly appear unless it can be seen that the structure effectively helps to make the Church a community of grace, a sacrament of Christ, a herald of salvation, and a servant of mankind.'[29]

Be that as it may, the model of Church as institution cannot be overlooked in our discussion, and we shall come to it in due course. For the moment, however, we must look more closely at some of the others. What I want to suggest is that the 'herald' and 'servant' models are especially helpful in disclosing aspects important for our theme. But the insights which they offer are balanced by those available through the model of the Church as sacrament.

Herald of Salvation

The model of the Church as herald resonates with the earliest New Testament conception, as we saw in reviewing the biblical data. A

Greek word for herald is *kerux*, which meant especially someone commissioned to pass on an official message: 'The basic image is that of the herald of a king who comes to proclaim a royal decree in a public square.'[30] The image is apt for one whose task it is to proclaim good news, and it is not surprising that the related word *kerygma* came to be used in reference to the core of the gospel proclamation. In proclaiming the kingdom Jesus was acting as herald, as were the earliest Christian communities when they proclaimed Jesus as Lord.

To look at the Church as herald is to see its mission primarily in terms of proclamation. Richard McBrien puts it in these words: '[The] mission of the Church is one of proclamation of the Word of God to the whole world. The Church cannot hold itself responsible for the failure of men to accept it as God's Word; it has only to proclaim it with integrity and persistence. All else is secondary. The Church is essentially a kerygmatic community which holds aloft, through the preached Word, the wonderful deeds of God in past history, particularly his mighty act in Jesus Christ. The community itself happens wherever the Spirit breathes, wherever the word is proclaimed and accepted in faith . The Church is event, a point of encounter with God.'[31]

In its stress upon the primacy of the Word this way of looking at the Church is, so to say, 'protestant', and it is no surprise to find that among its leading exponents are Karl Barth and Rudolf Bultmann. Its merits and demerits are indicated by Dulles, and he shows how in a 'catholic' ecclesiology it needs to be complemented by models which take account of such features of Church as its sacramentality, its universal (as well as local) character, its need of stable structure, and so on. We need not dwell on these now, for the significance of the model for us lies mainly in what it makes of the nature of gospel proclamation.

That proclamation, let it be reiterated, is that the reign of God's love has been inaugurated in the personal history of Jesus Christ. In his history the love is incarnated, in a literal sense made flesh, so that if we look at the history we see the love revealed. The love is grace, both in the sense that it is undue and in that it enhances our existence. It is a faithful love: God has kept his promise to Israel and his fidelity withstands humanity's waywardness. It is forgiving and it will not hold sin against whomever turns to God out of faith in the good news of salvation. We have seen that repentance includes a return to good living and that the kerygma was invariably accompanied by a *didache* which contained ethical directives: converts are 'to lead a life worthy of God, who calls you into his own kingdom and glory'.[32] But the good news is prior, and it is the basis of (indeed it *is*) an invitation to reciprocate God's love in faith, hope and charity. Jesus was not merely a moral teacher, and to see him as moral teacher only is to miss his essential significance. Gospel proclamation is not just a summons to good living, and to see it thus is to impoverish it. The early Church saw itself as heralding the kingdom, and to conceive it as just one more agency for the improvement of morality in the reforming atmosphere of the Graeco-Roman world is to misrepresent it radically.

So it is with the Church today. In historical continuity with its founder and his followers it is the herald of salvation for the world now. That means that its key task is to witness to the gospel of grace, of mercy and forgiveness. That task, as is stressed so often in the theology of the Council, is a task of the whole Church together. But inevitably it is a particular responsibility of the Church's hierarchical leadership.

We shall examine later the place of the hierarchy and how it fulfils its role. For now it is enough to observe that the theological priority of the fact of salvation and of salvation's proclamation establishes a point of reference for all Church preaching and teaching. Of course—in the act of announcing the gospel—there is always a call to repentance. And, as with the prophets of the old dispensation and the apostles of the new, there will always be challenge to better living, and direction as to how this may be achieved. But if the Church is to be faithful to its raison d'être, neither challenge nor direction may obscure the absolute priority of the news that the Lord is compassion and love.

Servant of the Word and World
A second model which, in view especially of its explicit external reference, is apt for us is that of the Church as servant. We saw that *Gaudium et Spes* portrays the Church as sharing 'the joy and hope and grief and anguish of the people of our time', and as cherishing 'a feeling of deep solidarity with the human race and its history'.[33] And the Council, 'as witness and guide to the faith of the whole people of God, gathered together by Christ, can find no more eloquent expression of its solidarity and respectful affection for the whole human family, to which it belongs, than to enter into dialogue with it . . .'.[34] The Church 'is not motivated by earthly ambition but is interested in one thing only - to carry on the work of Christ under the guidance of the Holy Spirit, for he came into the world to bear witness to the truth, to save and not to judge, to serve and not to be served'.[35]

Dulles summarises the model's significance accordingly:

The Church's mission, in the perspectives of this theology, is not primarily to gain new recruits for its own ranks, but rather to be of help to all men, wherever they are. The special competence of the Church is to keep alive the hope and aspiration of men for the Kingdom of God and its values. In the light of this hope the Church is able to discern the sign of the times and to offer guidance and prophetic criticism. In this way the Church promotes the mutual reconciliation of men and initiates them in various ways into the Kingdom of God.[36]

Of the herald model Dulles has observed that it is one of those which 'give a primary or privileged position to the Church with respect to the world'.[37] Indeed he goes so far as to say that in it 'the Church takes on an authoritarian role, proclaiming the gospel as a divine message to which the world must humbly listen'.[38] This is putting the point somewhat strongly—and 'authoritative' seems a better term than 'authoritarian' to describe the herald's stance and tone. (The fact that Church authority sometimes appears as authoritarian is another matter.) It is however true that in this conception the Church is bringing something to the world which the world as such does not possess - the good news of the salvation in Jesus Christ. And this may beget a complacency or a sense of superiority on the part of Christians.

The image of servant helps to counteract that risk. The Church is servant of both the gospel and the world, and so it is neither above the gospel nor over against the world. Although, as Dulles says, there is no direct biblical foundation for the use of the image precisely as model of the Church, it is apt in that it evokes the scriptural portrayal of Jesus himself as Suffering Servant. And it is immediately congenial to the situation of the individual Christian as well as to that of the corporate Church: indeed it is perhaps easier to see how each of us is servant than to appreciate how we are each herald.

In a review of usage of the servant model Dulles cites a pastoral letter of the late Cardinal Cushing which portrays the Church as the body of Christ the Suffering Servant: 'So it is that the Church announces the coming of the Kingdom not only in word, through preaching and proclamation, but more particularly in work, in her ministry of reconciliation, of binding up wounds, of suffering service, of healing.'[39] In this perspective the Church is *in* the world and *with* it, and in an attitude of ministry rather than of lordship. Its character is well caught in a sentence of Dulles which describes the 'beneficiaries' of the Church's action when it comports itself thus, as 'all those brothers and sisters the

world over, who hear from the Church a word of comfort or encourage-
ment, or who obtain from the Church a respectful hearing, or who
receive from it some material help in their hour of need'.[40]

The Church as Sacrament

But to conceive oneself as servant is not to be exempt from the risk of
self-importance or self-righteousness; 'Yr. Humble Servant' of an earlier
epistolary style was about as reliable a guide to actual demeanour as our
'Yours sincerely'. It is therefore salutary to have an eye also to another
way of looking at the Church which, as well as being richly suggestive
in itself, may help counter the hazards involved in both of the models
just examined. This is the model of Church as sacrament.

A definition of sacrament familiar from the catechisms is 'sign and
instrument of grace'. These somewhat abstract words mask what is an
essentially simple idea: that of a visible manifestation of the loving
presence of God. In Catholic theology, since the Council of Trent
especially, its usual application was to the seven liturgical 'moments'
called baptism, confirmation, eucharist, penance, extreme unction, holy
orders and matrimony. But modern theology has recovered an earlier
usage whereby Christ was said to be the sacrament of God, on the basis
that he was, in an exact sense, the embodiment or incarnation of God's
gracious love.[41] And as the Church's work makes Christ present now,
the Church in turn is called the sacrament of Christ.

Henri de Lubac was a pioneer in the modern exploration of this
insight and in its extension to ecclesiology, and the core meaning of the
latter development is well expressed in these words of his: 'If Christ is
the sacrament of God, the Church is for us the sacrament of Christ; she
represents him, in the full and ancient meaning of the term, she really
makes him present. She not only carries on his work, but she is his very
continuation, in a sense far more real than that in which it can be said
that any human institution is its founder's continuation.'[42]

Clearly this is a rich theme though we cannot here pursue it beyond
noticing one or two obvious implications. The Church is called to be a
sign of the love of God in the world. In Dulles' words again, 'it must
signify in a historically tangible form the redeeming grace of Christ'.[43]
And so, as Dulles remarks, 'it stands under a divine imperative to make
itself a convincing sign'.[44] It appears most fully as a sign, he continues,
'when its members are evidently united to one another and to God
through holiness and mutual love, and when they visibly gather to
confess their faith in Christ and to celebrate what God has done for

to sinners a call to repentance, a call to turn around and go back to
the Place whence we have come.

The community called Church is also servant, of the gospel and of
the world. It is servant of the gospel for it is meant to promote the reign
of which it is herald. And it is servant of the world for it is the world
which is to be restored through the power of the gospel. The reign of
God is a reign of love; and God's love is at work in the search for justice
and truth and peace, and all the other constituents of the 'holiness' to
which humanity is called. The Church is *in* the world and *with* it,
minister and not lord.

But the Church is also sacrament, sign and agent of the grace which it
proclaims. It is this most intensely when gathered in the communion of
the eucharist, and at the other moments of christian existence which
tradition has recognised as sacraments. But it is sacrament in a prior and
more general sense; for, mystical body of Christ as well as new People of
God, it renders Christ present in the world from age to age. And the
Church from age to age is called to live up to its own sacramentality.

Finally, the Church is an institution, which means among other
things that it has a constitution, a set of rules and a governing body.
And, making due allowance for Dulles' observations about the limi-
tions of this model, we shall have to consider some of its implications
in the next chapter. But we must now recall again that the entire
significance of the institutional elements of the Church resides in their
reference to the Church's meaning and mission.

them in Christ'.[45] It goes without saying that the Church
always live up to its sacramental calling.

We may say that if the Church is to be true to its sacrame
must seek to make visible the grace of which it is instrume
when it speaks of love or truth or justice it must also *be* lo
truthful and just. 'The offices and rituals of the Church must
appear as the actual expressions of faith, hope, and love of livi
Otherwise the Church would be a dead body rather than
Christian community. It would be an inauthentic sign—a sign
thing not really present, and therefore not a sacrament.'[46]

We normally ask that people practise what they preach, and
straightforward sense we should expect Christians, as individual
community, to live by the values of their gospel. But in the ligh
doctrine of the sacramentality of the Church the springs of C
responsibility are revealed as even deeper. For if the Church is sa
of Christ in the world *its own nature requires* that it embody th
religious and moral, which it preaches and to which it ministers

This is at once a summons and a judgment. Clearly it is a sui
in the vision which it offers of a community meant in the divin
to be a light to the world. But it is also always a judgment, for o
the Church in history is never perfectly what it is called to be
very being of the Church in the world therefore there is an exig
humility and a permanent need for repentance.

We must now bring together the principal insights which
derived, albeit sketchily, from Avery Dulles' elaboration of th
models of the Church. It may be remembered that Dulles stres
the models are complementary and that none is to be 'canonise
measure of the rest. Yet it seems right to say that the most basi
of the Church as communion. For the Church in its esse
community of people united in the faith that Jesus is Lord;
spiritual communion which this betokens—with each other a
God—is 'signified and engendered by an external commu
profession of the faith, discipline and sacramental life'.[47]

The lordship of Jesus is gospel (good news), for to speak of
Lord is another way of saying that in him is salvation at hand.
Church is charged with spreading the gospel, with making the
aware of the gracious gift of God. So the Church is herald of s
with the message that the reign of God has begun and its
triumph assured. God's reign is a reign of love and its proclan
a summons to loving, for love calls forth love. But a summons

5

'THE CHURCH TEACHES'

Among the models of the Church considered by Avery Dulles there is one which in his view should not be taken as primary. This is the model of institution[1] which envisages the Church in terms of its organisation and especially its governing structure. We earlier adverted to words of B.C. Butler which summarise it exactly: the Church is a society, with 'a constitution, a set of rules, a governing body, and a set of actual members who accept this constitution and these rules as binding on them . . .'[2] The reason why the institutional aspect cannot be primary is that it exists only to express and serve a prior reality, the work of salvation in Jesus Christ.

But institutionalisation is an inevitable feature of any enterprise if it is to endure. When people come together for a common purpose it is natural for them to organise even if only in an elementary way. Objectives are defined and the means of their achievement selected, a leadership emerges, some ground rules are adopted. So even if Jesus had left no detailed prescription for the Church's organisation and government it would be foolish to think that it could survive or its purposes prosper without an appropriate structure.

However the institutional elements are secondary to the nature of the enterprise. The membership of a football club exists not for the sake of the club committee but for the sake of playing the game. Procedural and other rules are meant to facilitate the club's objectives, not the private interests of any member or group. When leaders and led are no longer one in a common pursuit disintegration ensues; and obsession with rule for its own sake brings paralysis.

When undue prominence is accorded to the institutional there is danger of distortion of the meaning of Church, which is why theology has never for long been happy with a view which puts that dimension in the first place. Yet a tendency to accentuate the institutional has been a recurrent feature of Catholic theology since the sixteenth century. There were several reasons for this, but basically it may be said to reflect a preoccupation with aspects of ecclesial reality which the reformers belittled or denied.

So for example the visibility of the Church was stressed against those who would see it as an invisible community of the saved. The visible marks of community became important accordingly, and there was an emphasis on credal and dogmatic formulae, on ritual, and on juridically constituted structures of government: emblematic of unity in, respectively, faith, worship and government. And when the reformers spoke of the general priesthood of the faithful at the expense of the notion of a special ministerial priesthood the Council of Trent replied by defining the hierarchical constitution of the Church.[3]

We saw that the Second Vatican Council retrieved the proper context of church institutions, presenting them as meant to serve the gospel and the world. And Avery Dulles says that the institutional model can never be primary. But neither may the institutions be discounted, for they are an important aspect of the Church's presence in and to the world. This is perhaps especially true of one facet of church government, the teaching function. For in teaching, church leaders impinge not only upon church members but—partly through their effect upon the members, partly through being as it were overheard by others—also on the wider society.

Preaching the Gospel, Teaching the Faith

We must therefore now examine the Catholic Church's understanding of its teaching role especially in regard to morality. *Magisterium* is a familiar word in this context. It means in the first place the office—or role or function—of teacher but is often used to refer to the holders of that office, so that 'the *magisterium*' comes to mean the pope and the bishops as the ultimate bearers of teaching authority and responsibility in the Church.

Teaching has been an aspect of church leadership from the beginning, as we saw when we looked at the way in which the gospel was first spread. *Kerygma* or proclamation was at the heart of the process of conveying the word of salvation: The kingdom is at hand, Jesus is Lord, Christ has died, has risen, will come again. But it was necessary to explain what this meant, to draw out the meaning of the core proclamation; and *didache,* an explanatory or expository kind of teaching, was an invariable accompaniment of gospel preaching. This included instruction concerning the way of life appropriate to a follower of Christ, often called *paraenesis.*

It is as well to mention now, for we shall have reason to refer to it later, that there is another function in regard to morality: that which, following biblical terminology, may be called prophetic. This is yet another word whose usage in English may mislead for we think of prophecy as foretelling the future. But in the Bible a prophet was someone who spoke for God, or in God's behalf, addressing some concrete situation of injustice or other immorality, and confronting it with the burning word of God's anger, calling for conversion. The prophet did not usually reason or argue or try to apportion blame; he simply declared the wrongness of *this* situation and called for a change *now*. The prophetic mode is found especially in books such as those of Isaiah, Ezekiel and Amos; but John the Baptist was a prophet too, and some of the preaching of Jesus exemplifies the genre also.

Of course preaching and teaching are carried out in the Church by people other than the pope and the bishops; nor, increasingly nowadays, are these functions reserved to clergy. But in the Roman Catholic tradition ultimate teaching authority resides in the pope and bishops. Our main interest is in the relatively restricted question of the exercise of the bishops' teaching role at the level of the local Church, and that in connection mainly with ethical matters. But it may be helpful if we approach it by way of a review of some points of doctrine concerning the exercise and reception of *magisterium* generally.

We cannot enter into detail concerning the way in which the rudimentary leadership structures of the earliest literature assumed the shape found today in the institutions of the episcopate and the papacy nor can we attempt a detailed account of the development of *magisterium*.[4] It must suffice to say that the Council of Trent and the First Vatican Council between them defined certain essentials: the hierarchical constitution of the Church,[5] apostolic succession,[6] the primacy of Peter and of his successors,[7] and infallibility of the pope.[8] But we must also recall that the Second Vatican Council put these doctrines in context, and in particular that it pointed up the collegial character of church government; and it made it plain that all office in the Church is meant for service not lordship.

Magisterium in the Church

Some passages from *Lumen Gentium* will help us to move from a general sense of the nature and scope of *magisterium* towards particular items of doctrine which are important for our theme.

> Among the more important duties of bishops that of preaching the gospel has pride of place. For the bishops are heralds of the faith, who draw new disciples to Christ; they are authentic teachers, that is, teachers endowed with the authority of Christ, who preach the faith to the people assigned to them, the faith which is destined to inform their thinking and direct their conduct; and under the light of the Holy Spirit they make that faith

shine forth, drawing from the storehouse of revelation new things and old(cf. Mat 13:52); they make it bear fruit and with watchfulness they ward off whatever errors threaten their flock(cf. 2 Tim 4:14).[9]

This description of *magisterium* is all of a piece with what we have seen regarding kerygma and catechesis in the early Church: teaching is an aspect of the task of preaching the gospel. But what is the status of that teaching, and how is it meant to be received?

Bishops who teach in communion with the Roman Pontiff are to be revered by all as witnesses of divine and Catholic truth; the faithful, for their part, are obliged to submit to their bishops' decision, made in the name of Christ, in matters of faith and morals and to adhere to it with a ready and respectful allegiance of mind.[10]

At first sight this looks like nothing more than a fairly general characterisation: episcopal teaching is entitled to reverence and respect. In fact however the passage contains two technical expressions whose precise significance is a matter of the utmost importance. The first of these is the expression 'faith and morals', the second 'a ready and respectful allegiance of mind'. But before exploring the meaning of these phrases it will be useful to summarise the essential theology of the hierarchy's competence to teach. (I mean competence primarily at this point in a formal sense.)

This competence resides in two subjects, the pope and the college or body of bishops in communion with the pope. *Lumen Gentium* puts it thus:

. . . the Roman Pontiff, by reason of his office as Vicar of Christ, and as pastor of the entire Church, has full, supreme and universal power over the whole Church, a power which he can always exercise unhindered. The order of bishops is the successor to the college of the apostles in their role as teachers and pastors, and in it the apostolic college is perpetuated. Together with their head, the Supreme Pontiff, and never apart from him, they have supreme and full authority over the universal Church; but the power cannot be exercised without the agreement of the Roman Pontiff.[11]

When the pope teaches as it were routinely in the day-to-day exercise of his office his *magisterium* is said to be 'ordinary'; as is that of the bishops when, though dispersed throughout the world but in communion with the pope, they teach in matters of faith and morals. The papal *magisterium* is 'extraordinary' when the pope speaks *ex cathedra*, that is formally as head of the universal Church, proposing a doctrine to be held as a matter of the faith. The bishops may exercise an extraordinary *magisterium* when, convoked by the pope and together with him, they meet in ecumenical council.[12]

When the pope speaks *ex cathedra*—as, for example, Pope Pius XII did in 1950 when he defined the dogma of the Assumption of the Blessed Virgin—he is said to speak infallibly. A Council's teaching is not *per se* infallible but only when in regard to 'faith and morals' it deliberately purports to be. (It may be remembered that the Second Vatican Council deliberately refrained from the formal definition of doctrines.) We shall come in a moment to what is meant by saying that the pope or the episcopate teach 'infallibly', but first notice another important attribution of infallibility.

> Although the bishops, taken individually, do not enjoy the privilege of infallibility, they do, however, proclaim infallibly the doctrine of Christ on the following conditions: namely, when, even though dispersed throughout the world but preserving for all that, among themselves and with Peter's successor, the bond of communion, in their authoritative teaching concerning matters of faith and morals, they are in agreement that a particular teaching is to be held definitively and absolutely.[13]

So doctrine to be regarded as infallibly taught may emanate from one of three sources: the pope, speaking *ex cathedra* ; a Council when it purports to define solemnly a truth as being 'of the faith'; and the episcopate in communion with the chief bishop 'when they are in agreement that a particular teaching is to be held definitively and absolutely'. This last kind of teaching is also sometimes said to be the product of 'unanimity of the episcopal magisterium', and it is said to be recognisable by virtue of its having been taught *semper et ubique et ab omnibus,* a phrase which goes back to the fifth century.

But what does infallibility mean? John T. Ford provides a summary account: 'Roman Catholics generally understand infallibility as a divinely given assistance, implied in Christ's promise to send the Holy Spirit to his apostles and their successors to enable them to believe and to teach without error those truths that are necessary for salvation. Thus, acceptance of the church's infallibility is basically a faith-commitment that presupposes that God provides the church with effective means both for faithfully believing and authoritatively proclaiming the authentic message of the Gospel.'[14] It is important to notice that infallibility is in the first place a charism of the Church as a whole and that this is the context of the infallibility of the organs of *magisterium.*

An important practical aspect of the doctrine of infallibility is expressed in the teaching of the First Vatican Council that a doctrinal definition arising from the exercise of infallible *magisterium* is 'irreformable'. The exact meaning of this is a subject of discussion among ecclesiologists, but we shall not be too far wrong if we think of it as meaning that the essential insight conveyed in a definition may never be discarded. It does not mean that the insight in question may never be supplemented so as to disclose its meaning more amply or more profoundly. So, for example, the primacy of the papal office as defined by the First Vatican Council may be seen in a new light if considered in conjunction with the doctrine of collegiality. And it may be that a formula will in time be found which expresses the amended insight more precisely.

It is time now to return to the two technical expressions already specially noticed, 'faith and morals' (in reference to the subject-matter of the hierarchy's teaching competence) and 'a ready and respectful allegiance of mind' (in reference to the reception of teaching in the Church).

'Faith and Morals'

The expression 'faith and morals' in reference to the purview of the *magisterium* was put in currency in a formal way through the definitions of the First Vatican Council concerning infallibility. But the origin of the phrase is earlier: it was also used by the Council of Trent, and was indeed by then already known in theology.[15] Apparently, though, 'morals' did not, even at Trent, have the precise signification which it has for us. *Mores* was understood in its earlier more general sense to mean way (or ways) of life, and it included matters of church discipline and even of liturgical practice.

Vatican I evidently wished to make the point that the subject matter of the Church's competence to teach includes the requirements of the Christian way of life. What was not discussed, though it was briefly raised, was the question whether there were any differences between the character of *magisterium* in the realm of faith and its character in the realm of morality.

The reason that this question arises is obvious if we recall what we saw about the nature of morality: that it is a universal human enterprise founded in the nature of human being in the world, its prescriptions in principle accessible to anyone of good will. A matter of morality is therefore a matter of reason in a way in which a doctrine of the faith— whose origin is ultimately in revelation—is not.

Nor did the Council formally tackle the question what exactly is meant by 'morals' here? Is it morality in the sense in which we usually now think of it—prescinding therefore from, say, church discipline or ritual prescription? And if so, does it refer to the general principles of morality or to concrete applications? Does magisterial competence go to matters of the 'natural law', or is it confined to material (supposing there be such in the realm of morality) for knowledge of which we are indebted to the revelation which culminated in the personal history of Jesus Christ?

It is safe to suppose that at the least the Council must have wanted to assert a competence concerning morality in what is now the usual sense of the term—concerning, that is, the practice of the art of right relationship with each other and the world around us. But that brings us back to an earlier question: is there anything specifically Christian about this? If not, why should there be an exclusive competence on the part of hierarchy in this domain?

There has been much discussion of the question whether the *magisterium* is competent at all in matters of the natural law.[16] Some theologians have taken the view that it is not unless the material in question is also part of revelation. Others have considered that the natural law is itself revealed, inasmuch as it has been as it were adopted by Scripture and in the tradition of the Church; and the *magisterium* is accordingly competent to interpret and declare it. Others have denied any competence.

Modern discussion of this question has been conducted on the whole in terms inherited from the way in which it was seen in late nineteenth-century theology. In particular it has been envisaged in terms of the theology of nature and grace associated with the neo-scholastic movement of that period: in terms, that is, which made a sharp distinction between the realms of nature and grace, revelation and reason, the natural and supernatural orders. These distinctions are real; but a more modern theology has been insisting that they should not mislead us into false dichotomies. Grace presupposes nature and enhances it, the data of revelation are expressed in the language and forms of human communication. There are not two orders but rather one 'new creation', arena of the saving action of the God of Jesus Christ.[17]

In this light much of the discussion about the scope of the competence of *magisterium* appears as misconceived. For in theological reality there is no longer a purely 'natural' law but the law of nature graced. And when reason is informed by faith, when the believer and the community of believers reason within the horizons disclosed in the revelation, their subject is humanity as it is: humanity enhanced, but humanity for all that. It remains convenient, even in theology, to speak of 'natural' law, for continuing access to moral knowledge is through reflection on the kind we are, in the world which we inhabit: reflection, that is, on human nature and on all that is meant by creation. If there is a magisterial competence in morals—and we have seen why there must be—it cannot but involve itself in that reflection.

Just how it does this and to what effect is of course a different matter. I have suggested that much discussion of the scope of *magisterium* as regards the natural law has been flawed by faulty theological premises. By the same token the real question has been obcured. For the question lying behind a good deal of theological exchange upon this topic concerns the reach of magisterial competence so far as *concrete* moral guidance is concerned. Even when it is granted (or perhaps especially when it is granted) that its role necessitates recourse to what is recognisably a natural law methodology, how far can *magisterium* go in binding conscience?

But this is a question less about the theology of morals than about the logic of moral discourse and the attributes of different kinds of moral principle. What I mean is that its answer is to be sought not only in theological claims about the Petrine office or the apostolic succession or Christ's promise of the Spirit's assistance, relevant to the answer though these must be. But we must seek the answer to the question also in the nature of morality and of moral knowledge, and the ways in which we come to moral judgment.

It is therefore relevant to ask not only whether a moral imperative is contained in the Scripture or in the tradition of the Church but whether it is the sort of imperative that can be said to bind us still. Paul told slaves to be subject to their masters. Does that hold now? Why not—if not? Jesus told us to love the enemy. Does that hold now? Why—or why not? Are there times or places when a commandment is 'suspended'? Are there exceptions to some rules? Is there a difference between different kinds of imperative so that some can never change even if others can? How would you know which?

G.B. Guzzetti has written: '. . . there are two rather different kinds of moral norms. One type is made up of immutable eternal principles, of prescriptions which are valid always and everywhere for every situation of life. The other type has to do with applications that can and should change. The two types must be clearly and accurately distinguished. Otherwise there is a danger that mere applications, which should vary in time and space, will be defended as immutable, eternal norms. Or, on the other side of the coin, there is a danger that true and strict principles, which are universally and eternally valid, will be considered as bound to certain limits of time and space.'[18]

Our approach to the task here indicated is guided in part by criteria enunciated in the the Constitution *Dei Verbum* on divine revelation; the passage is important enough to merit quotation in full.

Seeing that in sacred Scripture God speaks though men in human fashion, it follows that the interpreter of sacred Scriptures, if he is to ascertain what God has wished to communicate to us, should carefully search out the meaning which the sacred writers really had in mind, that meaning which God had thought well to manifest through the medium of their words.

In determining the intention of the sacred writers, attention must be paid *inter alia* to literary forms, for the fact is that truth is differently presented and expressed in the various types of historical writing, in prophetical and poetical texts and in other forms of literary expression. Hence the exegete must look for that meaning which the sacred writer, in a determined situation and given the circumstances of his time and culture, intended to express and did in fact express through the medium of a contemporary literary form. Rightly to understand what the sacred writer wanted to affirm in his work, due attention must be paid both to the customary and characteristic patterns of perception, speech and narrative which prevailed at the age of the sacred writer, and to the conventions which the people of his time followed in their dealings with one another.[19]

What the Council is saying is that access to the meaning of what is expressed in the biblical books is through standard principles of interpretation which have regard to form and context and the laws of language. And the same could be said, *mutatis mutandis,* of other documents of the tradition.

The Council was speaking of theological truth in general but what it says applies to ethical doctrine, from the Bible or from the tradition, as well. And there is reason for particular care with moral teaching, for some of it is *of its nature* time-bound and rooted in a particular culture. Such is the case with what we earlier called material principle: specific concrete norms which aim to direct what people actually *do.* Telling women to keep silent in church was not incongruous in the Graeco-Roman world of the first century; it is now. The stipulation of the classical teaching concerning the 'just war' that non-combatants should not be killed answered to a situation when combatants were those who fought on a battlefield; it is meaningless in the context of all-out nuclear war.

Such is the circumstantial character of concrete moral teaching that many theologians say that it is impossible to universalise a negative material norm, that is a norm which forbids a determinate act—say killing or taking someone else's property without his or her consent. What they mean is that you cannot judge an act of that kind without taking circumstances and the mind of the person acting into account as well.[20] And since it is impossible to anticipate every possible combination of circumstance and motive/intention they conclude that it is not feasible to hold that there are concrete norms which always bind, to which there cannot be exceptions, which are not open to change. This is controversial, for in the Catholic tradition there are universal prohibitions which at least look like material norms: examples are the prohibition of lying, fornication, adultery, and of the direct killing of the innocent.[21]

I say 'at least look like' material norms, for some have thought it possible to question whether this is what they are. This view so defines the actions listed here that they include a moral term (lying is deception of someone not entitled to the truth, fornication is sexual intercourse outside the only context in which it makes moral sense). But this is to remove the norm *by definition* from the realm of the merely material; and it does not seem at all plausible in the case of some of the prohibitions, notably that of artificial contraception. Another approach has followed a rubric of Aquinas in saying of certain norms that they hold in most cases ('valent ut in pluribus')[22] or, in a more modern terminology, that they are 'virtually absolute'.[23] But this concedes their non-universalisability, at least as a matter of theory.

An implication of this is that it is difficult to speak meaningfully about infallibility in morals, at least if an infallibly taught doctrine is envisaged in terms of its irreformability. For, as we have already seen, moral statements are of three main kinds: formal, tautologous and material. Now a formal statement, if it is true at all, is timelessly true: it is impossible to imagine an exception to the principle that justice must be done. A tautology is necessarily true: it makes no sense to say that murder is sometimes justified. And we have just seen that there are substantial theoretical difficulties about universalising a material norm. Hence an ascription of irreformability in virtue of the exercise of the charism of infallibility is either redundant—as in the cases of formal and tautologous norms—or, by the logic of moral discourse, problematic.

There is a way in which it might make sense to speak of infallible teaching in the moral domain, and that is if regard is had not to the scope of a norm but to the question whether it belongs to the 'stock' of Christian principles or not. In that case it might be said that the primacy of the love commandment, or the notion of equality or personal dignity, or the principle that justice must be done are taught infallibly as pertaining to the Christian moral vision, and that none can ever be dropped from the stock of norms and notions which comprise the Christian code. But this, plainly, is a different concept of irreformability than is in question when one speaks of the irreformability of moral norms.

All in all then the application of the doctrine of infallibility to the teaching of morals is problematic. And that may be part of the reason that there is no instance of a solemn definition of concrete moral doctrine in the history of the *magisterium*. Some theologians hold, however, that there are concrete moral truths which must be considered infallibly taught in virtue of the infallibility of the ordinary *magisterium*. But this thesis too seems difficult to sustain, for the same reasons as in the case of extraordinary *magisterium*: propositions which are formal or tautologous are in any case timelessly true, and it seems that merely material propositions are not universalisable.

'Obsequium Religiosum'

But the fact that a doctrine may not be taught irreformably does not mean that it can be disregarded, as is indicated in the passage from *Lumen Gentium* quoted above when it speaks of 'a ready and respectful obedience of mind'. This point is made even more clearly in the sentence following: 'This loyal submission of will and intellect must be given in a special way to the authentic teaching authority of the Roman Pontiff, even when he does not speak *ex cathedra*, in such wise, indeed, that his supreme teaching authority be acknowledged with respect, and that one sincerely adhere to decisions made by him . . .'[24]

Notice here the word 'authentic'. It is possible to be misled by this too if we stick too closely to English usage, for in English the word usually carries an implication of truthfulness or genuineness. In our context however it is in the first place a synonym for 'authoritative'. Of course we should expect authoritative teaching to be truthful also, and we may expect that such teaching is as a rule true. The point is that its truth is not guaranteed in the absolute way in which the truth of an infallibly taught statement is.

But if the Spirit's assistance is to have any practical effect there is surely a presumption of truth in the authoritative utterances of the ordinary *magisterium*. And this is the basis for the requirement that such teaching should be received with the attitude characterised as 'ready and respectful obedience of mind' and often summarised in the expression *obsequium religiosum*.[25]

There has been much discussion of the meaning of this expression, especially in the debate which followed the publication of *Humanae Vitae* in 1968. The nub has been the question, under what conditions, if at all, may a Catholic dissent from authoritative teaching? The essence of an answer was worked out in the nineteenth and early twentieth centuries in the wake of the definitions concerning primacy and infallibility and during the controversy which accompanied the modernist movement in the Church. The lines of that answer are still offered by the most authoritative writers though it is considered that the response needs to be modified in the light of more modern circumstances.[26]

Central in the response is the contention that, although it must be regarded as highly exceptional, it is in principle licit to differ with a doctrine which does not purport to be an instance of infallible teaching. But a dissenting view would have to be grounded in good argument and would presuppose that the holder was expert in theology, a requirement normally met only by an adequate theological education. It was emphasised that dissent should remain private so as to obviate disturbance in the Church. Scholars might communicate their difficulties among themselves, but not in a journal or other forum which was likely to be 'popularly' influential.

There is nothing mysterious about the main lines of this approach; it is indeed largely a matter of common sense. As already said, we should expect the considered and Spirit-assisted teaching of responsible leaders to enjoy a presumption of truth, a presumption not lightly to be overturned. Nor is it a particular benefit in the Christian community when the teaching of its tradition and its leaders is constantly questioned in virtue merely of the shifting circumstances of the times.

But it must be asked whether today it is either practical or desirable to insist upon confining questions whether to scholarly journals or to the private meetings of theologians. It is virtually impossible to do so in practice if only because the media now take an interest in the domestic business of the Churches, including discussion of theology. When theological and other religious journals are on public sale or when, as often happens, a journal is routinely sent to the religious affairs correspondents of newspapers or other media, it is no longer practical to expect that the existence of a question or difference be kept secret.

Nor, all things considered, is it desirable. For the faith and its ways are not the property of the leadership or of professional theologians but are a matter of the living experience of believers. Theology dies when its practice is severed from the faith-community's experience, and the truthfulness of the experience is eventually jeopardised for want of reflection and a creative re-expression. *Magisterium* itself is put in jeopardy, for it cannot teach if it does not hear the questions. And there is a special hazard and a particular inappropriateness in seeking to restrict discussion of questions which arise in lay experience.[27]

6

TEACHING IN THE LOCAL CHURCH

The main elements of Catholic doctrine concerning *magisterium* in the Church have been summarised so as to provide the background for an examination of the kind of intervention which episcopal Conferences sometimes make in public debate about matters of social morality. It should now be possible to situate this kind of teaching so that its significance is neither overestimated nor overlooked.

Such teaching's significance is overestimated when it is taken to be as it were tinged with infallibility, or when its content is taken as inevitably belonging to the core of the faith. However, it may not be disregarded by one who wishes to be loyal to the Catholic inheritance, for it does possess authority. Nor, I shall argue, if it has to do with politics or law or economics, may it be written off on the basis that these areas are outside the scope of 'the faith'. But what kind of authority has it and what is its binding force?

It should perhaps be explained that the concept of an episcopal 'Conference' is new, at least in the way it is nowadays understood. Well before the Council the hierarchies of many countries met at intervals in order to canvas common problems and pursue common tasks. But following the Council and in the light of its ecclesiology 'collegial' action at national or regional level has come to assume a special significance. The nature of a Conference's authority as a matter of theology has been the subject of dispute; but no-one disputes the immense pastoral potential of what is now called the episcopal Conference.[1]

The Bishops' Conference, Faith and Morals

When a bishops' Conference speaks of matters of faith it may of course reproduce doctrine already held to be infallibly taught, and in that case it will look for the response of faith. Alternatively it may participate in ordinary *magisterium* as we have described it above. In that case it will offer authentic or authoritative teaching in the technical sense; or indeed in a given case its teaching may meet the criteria for infallible ordinary *magisterium*.

But what of 'morals'? And what in particular of areas such as politics or law or economics which have their own principles and procedures while being yet amenable to moral appraisal? Perhaps the first thing to stress is that these areas *are* amenable to comment from an ethical standpoint. The point is well made by the US Catholic Bishops' Conference in the course of a pastoral letter on the economy: it is perfectly in order from a moral point of view to ask what an economy is doing *to* people or *for* them.[2] And the question cannot be discounted on the basis that those who ask it are not professional economists, for its asking does not presuppose the economist's expertise.

It is moreover in order to point out that a particular system is, from a moral point of view, questionable, if such is the case. It is surely in order to say for instance that an economic system which characteristically corrects itself by penalising the already vulnerable—the sick or the young or those who depend upon 'welfare'—has *prima facie* a case to answer morally. An economist or a politician might want to say that to cut public spending is in a given case the only way to ameliorate a country's plight. But there remains the question: can it be right for a community to be content with a consistent recourse to measures whose effect is to make its poorer members poorer?

Of course when a critique goes further and offers alternatives, it is itself in turn open not only to continuing moral criticism but also to evaluation from within the field into which it has ventured. Its authority now presupposes a technical expertise and its solutions are subject to scrutiny in the light of the relevant canons of (say) economic theory. Someone who, lacking a grasp of the elements of a particular discipline, begins to prescribe solutions to complex problems in the field has only himself to blame when the wrath of the professional descends.

Response of the Faithful

But how are Catholics expected to receive this kind of teaching? Pope and bishops inherit the apostolic office and mandate, and their ministry is promised the assistance of the Spirit. What this means in practice for the authority of a bishops' Conference in matters of morality and law requires close and nuanced scrutiny.

I said earlier that it is a mistake to think of the sort of leadership which we are discussing as somehow tinged with infallibility. Leaving aside the difficulties inherent in giving an account of the meaning of infallibility in morals—not to mention its application to the teaching of an episcopal Conference—it is in any case a fact that much teaching in the arena of social morality is of the order of very local concrete application. The US Catholic Bishops' Conference displayed a keen consciousness of this in the pastorals on the economy and on war. While reiterating principles which belong to the core of Christian moral tradition the bishops were explicit in declining to make inordinate claims for the practical applications which the pastorals put forward.[3]

These concrete applications are judgments which presuppose a knowledge of the facts and an awareness of the horizons of the disciplines which concern themselves with the realities which the pastorals examine. So for example the letter on the economy works with factual data concerning poverty and unemployment in an effort to translate the moral requirement of social justice into concrete terms. It also employs analyses which presuppose certain views of economics and politics. Were it not to have made use of this kind of information its call to justice would have remained at a level of generality which did little to illuminate action. By using them it laid itself open to challenge from people who disagreed with the data or the methods and presuppositions of analysis.

General Principle or Specific Application?
But which is better—to speak of justice or of peace at a level of uncontrovertible generality, or to opt for more concrete critique and proposal at the risk of inviting disagreement and perhaps in the end refutation?

There is something to be said for the former mode.[4] For one thing there is no gainsaying the competence of the bearers of *magisterium* to declare the central principles of the Christian ethic. And indeed there are times and places where this suffices, the practical application of the principles being left to the judgment of people who opt to live in their light. Moreover this seems to accord with the notions of lay competence and responsibility and of the autonomy of secular affairs which the Second Vatican Council stressed.

A further consideration in favour of this mode of teaching arises from an observation made by *Lumen Gentium* when discussing the role of the layperson: 'Very often their Christian vision will suggest a certain solution in some given situation. Yet it happens rather frequently, and legitimately so, that some of the faithful, with no less sincerity, will see the problem quite differently. Now if one or other of the proposed solutions is too easily associated with the message of the Gospel, they ought to remember that in those cases no one is permitted to identify the authority of the Church exclusively with his own opinion.'[5]

Although these remarks refer to laity they are suggestive also for certain levels of clerical or hierarchical leadership. Precisely when *magisterium* moves into very concrete application of principle it is entering the realm of the controvertible. In part, as we have seen, this is because of the inherent character of material specifications of principle: remember Aquinas' passage about goods held in trust, remarked in the previous chapter.[6] Partly also, though, it is a consequence of the fact that practical judgments may involve interpretation and analysis the validity of which is a matter for the particular science or other disciplines concerned. If laity may not attribute an undue authority to what is an issue of legitimate difference of opinion neither may the bearers of official *magisterium*.

For all that, I think that the exercise of *magisterium,* if it is to be effective, will sometimes require that concrete problems are addressed and concrete solutions proposed. Being for justice in general terms is like being against sin—a worthy stance but of no help to someone who wants guidance on what to do. There are concrete norms of justice which, even if not exceptionless, yet hold in most cases, as the piece cited from Aquinas concedes. There are concrete situations in which a prophetic word, of hope or of excoriation, not hedged by reservation or qualified by otherwise desirable nuance, is what is needed to spur to change. And there are moral issues in relation to which the best service the bearers of *magisterium* can provide is to intitiate and enable debate.

This last will cause pause among those who expect *magisterium* always to say the last word. That expectation is sometimes linked with a false sense of the scope of the Spirit's assistance: with the belief, to put it roughly, that church hierarchy is omnicompetent and always infallible. It may also reflect misunderstanding about the nature of moral judgment, according concrete applications of principle a universality and conclusiveness which it is not in their nature to have.

An Example

The distinction at issue here—between the central and abiding insights of the Christian moral tradition on the one hand, and on the other the concrete specification of the ways in which these values may now be served—is illustrated clearly in the US bishops' pastoral on warfare. An early paragraph puts it thus:

> As Catholic bishops we write this letter as an exercise of our teaching ministry. The Catholic tradition on war and peace is a long and complex one; it stretches from the Sermon on the Mount to the

statements of Pope John Paul II. We wish to explore and explain the resources of the moral-religious teaching and to apply it to specific questions of our day. *In doing this we realise, and we want readers of this letter to recognise, that not all statements in this letter have the same moral authority* (italics mine).[7]

This is amplified in the sentences which follow:

At times we state universally binding moral principles found in the teaching of the Church; at other times the pastoral letter makes specific applications, observations which allow for diversity of opinion on the part of those who assess the factual data of a situation differently. However, we expect Catholics to give our moral judgments serious consideration when they are forming their own views on specific problems.[8]

Among the universally binding moral principles relied upon in the letter are that human life is always to be respected, and that the intentional killing of non-combatants is always wrong. And some concrete applications of these and other general principles are set out in the following paragraphs on the use of nuclear weapons:

1. *Counter Population Use:* Under no circumstances may nuclear weapons or other instruments of mass slaughter be used for the purpose of destroying population centres or other predominantly civilian targets. Retaliatory action which would indiscriminately and disproportionately take many wholly innocent lives, lives of people who are in no way responsible for reckless actions of their government must also be condemned.

2. *The Initiation of Nuclear War:* We do not perceive any situation in which the deliberate initiation of nuclear war, on however restricted a scale, can be morally justified. Non-nuclear attacks by another state must be resisted by other than nuclear means. Therefore, a serious moral obligation exists to develop non-nuclear defensive strategies as rapidly as possible. In this letter we urge NATO to move rapidly toward the adoption of a 'no first use' policy, but we recognise this will take time to implement and will require the development of an adequate alternative defense posture.

3. *Limited Nuclear War:* Our examination of the various arguments on this question makes us highly sceptical about the real meaning of 'limited'. One of the criteria of the just-war teaching is that there must be a reasonable hope of success in bringing about justice and peace. We must ask whether such a reasonable hope can exist once

nuclear weapons have been exchanged. The burden of proof remains on those who assert that meaningful limitation is possible. In our view the first imperative is to prevent any use of nuclear weapons and we hope that leaders will resist the notion that nuclear conflict can be limited, contained or won in any traditional sense.[9]

It will be seen that the very wording in these paragraphs is indicative of a variation in authority as between the several sorts of directive and observation which they contain. And it will come as no surprise to discover that reaction to their content varied also, including among members of the Catholic Church itself.

What of this? We have seen that the bishops expressly said that they expected Catholics to give 'serious consideration' to the bishops' moral judgments when making up their minds on the issues involved.[10] But they also made it wholly plain that even Catholics might differ upon some of the concrete applications, if only because of the possibility of a difference of intepretation of the factual data.

Free to Choose?

A similar kind of question has arisen for Catholics in Ireland at intervals during the past two decades when issues of morality and law have come up for public debate. As it has turned out, the bishops have evolved a characteristic way of addressing these issues. For when we study their statements we find that they embody both an affirmation of the right and responsibility of each voter to make up his or her own mind and a clear statement of the Conference's preferred position.[11]

The potential for tension here is a source of unease for many Catholics. They wish to be loyal to their tradition and its custodians, yet they must be loyal also to their own conscientious judgment. And, it has to be said, they are not accustomed to a sense of their own responsibility in matters of this kind. Critics have accused the bishops of trying to have it both ways, or of taking with one hand what they give with the other. Some see their line as symptomatic of a failure of nerve: they are no longer able or willing to speak out clearly on the side of Catholic beliefs. Others consider that the new mode is merely a slightly more sophisticated way of telling politicians and the electorate what to do. (Colour is lent to this interpretation whenever priests—and a few individual bishops—have insisted that there is in reality only one way for a loyal Catholic to vote.) Even among people sympathetic to the bishops' understanding of their duty to speak in these debates there are those who would wish them simply to affirm the principle that it is for each citizen or legislator to make up his or her own mind.

Now we have already seen that it is untrue that Catholic tradition obliges one to try to ensure the enforcement of Catholic moral beliefs by the law. Fornication is regarded by that tradition as immoral yet there is no call for its prohibition by the law of the land. Practicality of implementation, as in this example, is an obvious test of the wisdom of making a law; but so is the degree of moral consensus which a measure reflects, or with which it is likely to be backed. And of course people might agree on the moral value of a particular behaviour or state of affairs while differing on how best to support it by legislation. We shall return to these points later as we try to elaborate a framework in which this type of question may be treated. For the moment we need only notice again that it is simply not true that Catholicism enjoins the prohibition of every immorality by the law.

But what of the view that in any case the bishops are in the end trying to tell politicians what to do? Or the view which accepts that their affirmation of freedom of conscience is wholehearted but thinks its impact blunted when the bishops in fact take a side? Or what of someone who wants only to do 'the right thing'?

In any attempt to cope with questions of this kind some considerations are basic. First, everything that was said by the Vatican Council concerning the role of lay experience and expertise and the relative autonomy of secular affairs must be taken fully seriously. Second, due weight must always be accorded the distinctions alluded to above: between general moral principle and its specification in concrete terms and, even more particularly, between moral conviction and political judgment. A kind of augmented authority may not be claimed, covertly or otherwise, for judgments which are in principle debatable or revisable, even when these judgments are reached after extensive deliberation and reflection. Above all it is quite wrong to accuse someone of disloyalty to the faith for exercising his or her right to independent judgment in matters in which difference is legitimate.

What this comes down to, in the simplest terms, is that even the most strongly expressed teaching by an episcopal Conference cannot override the prior responsibility of each citizen to make up his or her own mind. Another way of putting the matter is this: the bishops' duty to lead the members of their Church includes a duty to speak on sociolegal matters which have moral import and they have a right to do so even if, outside their own people, they are regarded simply as just another interest group. And I have argued above that in principle they are not precluded from being quite specific, and indeed I have suggested that in appropriate cases effective leadership requires that they be specific. But the more they move from the substance of the faith the more they enter territory which merits the attribution of a legitimate autonomy according to Vatican II, and the more does lay competence come into its own. It is to be assumed that whatever specific positions they adopt are not lightly taken, and it would be foolish indeed to ignore the kind of argument which they make. Nevertheless it is the right as well as the responsibility of each citizen to put that argument in the balance (to use an expression of the Irish Conference)[12] and to come to his or her own conclusion.

It is therefore quite wrong for anyone to seek to tarnish a dissenting view by representing it as disloyal. It is especially perverse to do so when—as in the case of the Irish Conference's statements on matters of morality and law in recent decades or the US Bishops' pastorals on warfare and on the economy—the legitimacy of difference of opinion is expressly acknowledged by the bishops.

But what happens when a Conference feels strongly enough to make what amounts to a plea to follow the view which they espouse? An example of this is the US bishops' call to NATO 'to move rapidly toward the adoption of a "no first use policy" ', though they 'recognise this will take time to implement and will require the development of an adequate alternative defense posture'.[13] This is a position to which many subscribe and about which many feel a sense of moral urgency. Yet the principle enunciated above must be honoured: it remains wholly open to a Catholic to hold a differing view.

7

In Search of a Principle

The paradigm of the Church's preaching is the preaching of Jesus: The kingdom of God is at hand; repent and believe the Gospel.[1] Its message is first a religious message: that there is a provident and gracious God whose inbreak in history is a story of human salvation. There is a moral dimension: God's love asks ours, and we do not love Him if we do not love the neighbour. In fact we often fail, so the call to love is a call to repent, to gather ourselves up and begin again. But the last word is religious: repentance is grounded in the faith that in Christ is our salvation.

The Church is a community fashioned in that faith. It is herald of the reign of God, servant of the gospel of Jesus, sacrament of God's action in the world, presage of a coming glory. It is the whole Church which is called to this, each one's vocation to carry faith's spark so that the whole community of Christians is a light among the nations. Whenever the Christian vision is shrunken to a moral message it is distorted; when the work of the gospel is thought to be for leaders only the mission of the Church is impoverished.

It is against this background that engagement of the Church in and with 'the world' is to be seen. Church people will be concerned with moral value, but in the first place constructively, creatively, as zealous to see that justice is done as that injustice is undone. And moral concern is best nourished in lived experience, and the bearers of official *magisterium* will take care to hear experience's witness. They will acknowledge an 'autonomy of earthly affairs',[2] and will recognise also that it is to the laity, even if not exclusively to them, that secular duties and activity properly belong.[3]

There will be times when the Church must distance itself from the way the world is going: a community of Christians could not, for example, be at peace in a setting which exploited human needs or degraded human being. And there will be times when hierarchical leadership, overseeing the work of the gospel, finds it necessary to propose a stand in the name of

gospel values. There is a time for criticism and for the prophetic mode and
for the unmuffled voice of authoritative leadership. But the stance, individual or institutional, should never be selfrighteous or indifferent to the
sensibilities of others of good will. And never may this aspect of the
Church's task obscure its role as sacrament of salvation.

The Question

But the question which focuses the themes of this book is both more
precise and more mundane: how, when it comes to the embodiment of
a moral belief in the law, is a Catholic expected to vote? The foregoing
generalities are suggestive but can anything more concrete be said?

One way of approaching our question is to look again at the way in
which the Irish Episcopal Conference has intervened in debates of this
kind during the past two decades or so. The bishops have offered, as we
saw, both an affirmation of the right of the politician or voter to make
up his/her own mind on the issue, and a statement of the Conference's
view on the proposed measure. This stance has been a source of
puzzlement, for it has seemed to some to embody an inconsistency if
not a contradiction. If the issue is up to the voter's conscience why do
the bishops take a position? And if what they really want is to have their
view adopted why pretend that the question is open?

In fact the stance of the bishops is not at all mysterious. The affirmation of a freedom of judgment is based first on the distinction between a
moral belief and the embodiment of that belief in law and, second, on the
premise that the latter is a matter of civic or political judgment, the
province of citizen or politician as such, and about which there may be
difference of opinion. The expression of the Conference's view of the issue
is a right and duty of a body whose function, alike in their own theology
and in the public mind, involves a special concern for the common good.

We ourselves have already seen something of the differences between
morality and law and we have adverted to the question whether it is the
business of the law to enforce morality or, as it is sometimes also put, to
make immorality a crime. Later we shall see how that question has fared
in a famous modern debate, but we may as well notice now that it is by
no means new in the history of Christian thinking. For St Thomas
Aquinas considered it in the *Summa Theologiae* in the course of his tract
on law, and he cited among his authorities St Isidore and St Augustine.[4]
Aquinas asks both whether it is the law's function to make people virtuous
and whether it should forbid all vice. Here we must be content to notice a
few salient points in his response.

Aquinas, Morality and Law

Notice first his relative optimism concerning law's significance: he views it as a medium by which God 'builds us up'[5] in our progress into goodness. Notice also his exalted view of even man-made law. Having established the existence of an Eternal Law whereby 'the whole community of the universe is governed by God's mind', and of a Natural Law which is 'a sharing in the Eternal Law by rational creatures', he sees the law-maker's task as one of reasoning from Natural Law's principles to certain 'more specific arrangements', called human laws inasmuch as they 'fulfil the essential conditions of law already indicated'.[6] These conditions have been set out in an examination of the nature of law: it is an ordinance of reason, made in aid of the common good, by whomever has charge of the community, and promulgated.[7]

Here is a view of human law which links it not just with the moral law but with God's design for the whole creation. In that design each creature has its purpose, each moves toward its goal. 'Among [beings] intelligent creatures are ranked under divine Providence the more nobly because they take part in providence by their providing for themselves and others'.[8] The human creature's goal is God, toward whom we move drawn by grace but freely. The human role is therefore creative, constructive: men and women, under God, have to make something of themselves and of their world, discovering and respecting the divine design.

So in Aquinas' perspective the making of law is in service of virtue; and law is derived from [*derivetur*] morality in two ways. First it may be deduced, as a conclusion is deduced from a premise: for instance, 'You must not commit murder' can be inferred from 'You must do harm to nobody.'[9] Second, a law may be one of a number of alternative options for securing the realisation of a moral insight. So, for example, morality requires that crime be punished but it is for the lawmaker to choose the form which a punishment should take ('the punishment settled is like a determinate form given to natural law').[10]

This is important, for it shows that though law in Thomas' mind always 'translates' a moral viewpoint, it is not always as by direct and necessary inference. Another way of putting this is to say that a particular piece of legislation, though it embodies a moral insight, may not be the only way in which the insight is concretised; and there is room for debate concerning the appropriateness of any particular item of lawmaking. 'The first process [deduction] is like that of the sciences where inferences are demonstratively drawn from principles. The second process is like that of the arts, where a special shape is given to a general idea, as when an architect determines that a house should be in this or that style.'[11]

There is therefore an art of lawmaking and it is not the same as the art of the moralist, and its autonomy must be respected. This autonomy does not bespeak an indifference to morality: we have seen that both kinds of lawmaking render, even if in each case differently, an essentially moral insight. It does, however, mean that the moralist is not necessarily competent to say what the form of a law must be; and that whoever would do so must have regard to all the factors which may pertain to the care of a community in view of a common good.

Earlier I alluded to an optimism on the part of Aquinas concerning the place of law: it is one of the media which God may use to 'bring us up' [instruere] in virtue. And indeed he answers affirmatively the question, 'Is making men good an effect of law?'[12] At that point he is thinking of law in general, including God's law in its various forms, and not about the specific potential of human law, concerning which, as it turns out, his expectations are modest.

This question is first considered in a general way when he asks about the utility of man-made law. Although we have 'an innate bent' for virtue, yet 'to come to its fullness' we need education:

> Now for the young apt for deeds of virtue by good natural disposition or by custom or, better still, by divine gift, all that is required is the fatherly discipline of admonition. Not all the young, however, are like that; some are bumptious, headlong in vice, not amenable to advice, and these have to be held back from evil by fear and force, so that they at least stop doing mischief and leave others in peace. Becoming so habituated they may come to do of their own accord what earlier they did from fear, and grow virtuous. This schooling through the pressure exerted through the fear of punishment is the discipline of human law.[13]

Later he asks whether it is the business of human law to restrain all vice or enforce every virtue. It will be convenient if we take the second question first.

We have seen, says Thomas, that law is ordained to the common good, and in principle there is no virtue of which some activity cannot be prescribed by law. 'Nevertheless human law does not enjoin every act of every virtue, but those acts only which serve the common good, either immediately, as when the social order is directly involved from the nature of things, or mediately, as when measures of good discipline are passed by the legislator to train citizens to maintain justice and peace in the community.'[14]

But should the law try to restrain every vice? The core of the answer is no; for

> Law is laid down for a great number of people, of which the majority have no high standard of morality. Therefore it does not forbid all the vices, from which upright men can keep away, but only those grave ones which the average man can avoid, and chiefly those which do harm to others and which have to be stopped if human society is to be maintained, such as murder, theft and so forth.

Earlier he had observed that 'laws should be appointed to men according to their condition', and he quotes Isidore as remarking that law should be possible 'both according to the nature and the custom of the country'.[15] As we do not expect from a child the standard of virtue of an adult, so 'many things may be let pass in people of mediocre morals which cannot be countenanced in their betters'.[16]

Here the notion of law as educative is maintained but there is a realism about its potential. Aquinas accepts as a fact that the majority 'have no high standard of morality' and he believes that the law must be accommodated accordingly. A later passage amplifies: 'The purpose of human law is to bring people to virtue, not suddenly but step by step. Therefore it does not all at once burden the crowd of imperfect men with the responsibilities assumed by men of the highest character, nor require them to keep away from all evils, lest, not sturdy enough to bear the strain, they break out into greater wrongs.[17]

Thomas' attitude here is far from a modern recognition of pluralism of moral value: differences of moral belief and performance are rooted in waywardness, and the law's accommodations are necessitated by regrettable practical necessity.[18] The point to notice though is that he does not seek to impose ideal standards; nor does he expect the law to bring about virtue in a full sense.

But notice especially that he has distinguished between the art and concerns of the lawmaker and those of the moralist as such. Moral value is reflected in the law but the law's role is not the simple promotion of morals. There may be more than one way to express in concrete command and prohibition the requirements of humanity's flourishing, and it is for the lawmaker to discover which is the best. He will not try to enforce every possible virtuous activity nor repress all vice.

And notice also the pertinent criteria: law enjoins the kind of virtuous behaviour which serves the common good, 'either immediately, as when the social order is directly involved from the nature of things, or mediately, as when measures of good discipline are passed by the legislator to train citizens to maintain justice and peace in the community'.[19] And it prohibits chiefly those actions 'which do harm to others and have to be stopped if human society is to be maintained'.[20] Murder and theft are the only two examples given but they are perhaps sufficiently suggestive.

I have already intimated that it would be wrong to insinuate that Aquinas' standpoint is that of a modern, but its tenor and spirit are nonetheless instructive. It is well to be aware that at the heart of the tradition of Christian theologising on law there was considerable subtlety, founded in a sense of the practical and the humane. In serving morality law's prospects are modest: goodness cannot be forced. Lawmaking is always open to moral criticism but the priest may not usurp the ruler's role. Nor is there a Christian warrant for making law the medium of a tyranny of 'morals'.

The Second Vatican Council

But a modern will want a more 'modern' view of the issues. He or she may be uneasy about an apparent patronising of alternative viewpoint and practice. Not every dissent from Christian moral teaching is to be put down to a failure of intelligence or good will. Most people who seek divorce, for example, are neither morally retarded nor delinquent. What about 'pluralism', it will be asked, and the rights of minorities in a modern pluralist society?

Pluralism need mean no more than that there is a factual diversity of belief and practice in religious or moral matters in the world at large or within a particular community. In this sense there has always been a pluralism in morals, certainly in the world at large, and even in regions and countries. If our time is more aware of such diversity the reason is doubtless in modern possibilities for communication. I need only to allude to the 'revolution' in communications technology, and the relative facility with which a modern may travel the world.

And of course this awareness breeds questions for value systems if only by showing the viability—not to mention the rival attractions—of alternatives. In modern experience this combines with the democratic instinct so as to create a demand for the legitimation within communities of political or moral viewpoints hitherto looked on as deviant. If formerly the practical implementation of such a viewpoint was precluded by the law, the demand for its recognition now quite naturally takes the shape of a call for legal change.

A society or institution in which certain moral ideas and practices have been by tradition strongly held (or repudiated) will not readily respond to pressure for reform. So it is that countries in which a Roman Catholic tradition of morality has been influential have been slow to grant legal sanction to divorce (say) or abortion, for these are items concerning which the moral beliefs of Catholicism have been firm and clear. A similar point may be made about the legal situation of homosexuals, though in that case opposition to change has in some places been associated also with Christian Churches other than the Roman Catholic.

In making the case for a change in the law it is not enough to invoke a vague generalisation concerning the rights of minorities in a pluralist society. For there are minorities in our societies whose behaviour we should not dream of sanctioning by way of legal toleration: criminals for example, or subversives in the political order. It must be obvious that the mere fact that a belief is held by a minority, even a notable minority, is not enough to ground a case for change.

This is elementary—though sometimes apparently overlooked—and it is an obvious reason for the opposition of some people to arguments which appeal to pluralism. Another reason is that the appeal is thought to imply the view that one set of moral values is as good as another.[21] It is interesting to recall that a similar apprehension underlay resistance to the principle of what is usually called religious freedom, now a part of the official doctrine of the Catholic Church. But the *Declaration on Religious Freedom* of the Second Vatican Council makes it plain that religious indifferentism is not a necessary premise of the principle of religious freedom. Nor does conviction of the truth of one's own faith preclude an effective respect for the religious beliefs of others.

And it is to the doctrine of the Declaration that we now turn, in our search of a model for a resolution, in modern terms from a Roman Catholic standpoint, of the problem of the legal enforcement of morals. The teaching is found in a short document 'on the right of the person and communities to social and civil liberty in religious matters', entitled *Dignitatis Humanae*, and published by the Council on 7 December 1965.[22]

The teaching of the Council on religious freedom represented the maturation of ideas whose seedbed was the US experience of Catholicism and whose most eloquent exponent was the American Jesuit, John Courtney Murray. As articulated during the nineteenth century the official stance of Roman Catholicism *vis-à-vis* other faiths (or nonfaith) was at best one of grudging toleration. 'Error has no rights' was a basic maxim: ideally religious error should be proscribed, though in concrete circumstances it might be granted a provisional toleration for fear of greater evil. The core of the Council's achievement in regard to religious freedom was the replacement of this doctrine by one developed in the thought of Courtney Murray.[23]

The Declaration's starting-point is the modern consciousness of the dignity of the human person, and the growing demand that people 'should exercise fully their own judgment and a responsible freedom in their actions, and should not be subject to the pressure of coercion but be inspired by a sense of duty'.[24] This demand is 'concerned chiefly with . . . spiritual values, and especially with what concerns the free practice of religion in society'.[25] Attentive to these 'spiritual aspirations', the Council wishes to search church tradition 'from which it draws forth new things that are always in harmony with the old'.[26]

The Council then professes its belief that God's truth was revealed in Jesus Christ. It believes moreover that 'this one true religion continues to exist in the Catholic and Apostolic Church', to which the Lord gave the task of spreading it to all; and all have a duty to seek the truth, and to live by it as they come to know it.[27]

> The sacred Council likewise proclaims that these obligations bind [the] conscience. Truth can impose itself on the mind only in virtue of its own truth, which wins over the mind with both gentleness and power. So while the religious freedom which men demand in fulfilling their obligation to worship God has to do with freedom from coercion in civil society, it leaves intact the traditional Catholic teaching on the moral duty of individuals and societies toward the true religion and the one true Church of Christ.[28]

It is plain that the Council does not wish to diminish a whit the religious claims of the Catholic Church, or to lend any support to religious indifferentism. There is a revealed truth, it continues to maintain, to be found now in the faith of the Catholic Church, and everyone is bound to seek it out as best he or she may. Acknowledgment of a religious pluralism is not meant to suggest that one religion is as good as another. For all that, '[t]he Vatican Council declares that the human person has a right to religious freedom'.[29]

I shall argue later that though the Council's doctrine concerns religious (as distinct from moral) belief and practice, it affords guidance also in morality. But first let us see what it means and how the Council grounds it.

A Principle

> Freedom of this kind means that all should be immune from coercion on the part of individuals, social group and every human power so that, within due limits, nobody is forced to act against his convictions nor is

anyone to be restrained from acting in accordance with his convictions in religious matters in private or in public, alone or in association with others. The Council further declares that the right to religious freedom is based on the very dignity of the human person as known through the revealed word of God and by reason itself. This right of the human person to religious freedom must be given such recognition in the constitutional order of society as will make it a civil right.[30]

The principle therefore has two aspects: people should not be forced to act against their religious beliefs, nor should they be restrained from acting in their light; and this goes for the public as for the private domain. The qualification 'within due limits' is plainly of the greatest significance, and we shall have to return to it in a moment.

The basis for the principle is the dignity of the person, as known through divine revelation and by reason. 'It is in accordance with their dignity that all, because they are persons, that is beings endowed with reason and free will and therefore bearing personal responsibility, are both impelled by their nature and bound by a moral obligation to seek the truth, especially religious truth.'[31]

Human dignity resides in our being gifted with reason and freedom, and it belongs to our nature that we should look for the truth and live by it. 'But [people] cannot satisfy this obligation in a way that is in keeping with their own nature unless they enjoy both psychological freedom and immunity from external coercion.'[32] The right to religious freedom is founded not in the subjective attitude of the person but in human nature. 'For this reason the right to this immunity continues to exist even in those who do not live up to their obligation of seeking the truth and adhering to it.'[33] Again there is a practical corollary: 'The exercise of this right cannot be interfered with as long as the just requirements of public order are observed.'[34]

This is the second mention of a restriction of the exercise of the right to religious freedom: reference to 'the just requirements of public order' may be read as a gloss on the earlier expression 'within due limits'.[35] The concrete significance of the restriction is later indicated, in general and in particular. In general, 'in availing of any freedom [people] must respect the principle of personal and social responsibility; in exercising their rights individuals and social groups are bound by the moral law to have regard for the rights of others, their own duties to others and the common good of all'.[36] In particular, people's freedom is limited by the requirements of peace, justice and public morality, all of which are 'basic to the common good and [which] belong to what is called public order'.[37] After this fairly standard statement of the need to reconcile the enjoyment of rights with the facts of life in society the last word is given to freedom: 'For the rest, the principle of the integrity of freedom in society should continue to be upheld. According to this principle man's freedom should be given the fullest possible recognition and should not be curtailed except when and in so far as is necessary.'[38]

A Principle Transposed

I said earlier that as the Declaration is concerned with *religious* freedom as such, one needs to argue explicitly in favour of its application to morality.[39] Fortunately the argument is not complicated. For the principle of religious freedom is based on the dignity of the person and on the character of the search for truth, and these are the same whether one is thinking of morality or of religion. As gifted with reason and choice we live up to our dignity to the extent that we freely seek and live moral truth; and coercion is no more at home in the quest for moral than it is for religious value.

And so we may formulate a principle by analogy. In moral matters people should not be forced to act against their consciences nor should they be restrained from behaving according to conscience—provided that the just requirements of public order are observed. In morality as in religion there should be freedom of belief and action, in public and in private, for individuals and for groups, subject only to the requirements of peace, justice and public morality.

It hardly needs saying that our next business is with the force of the statement that freedom in matters of moral conscience is constrained by the requirements just mentioned. But it is perhaps worth remarking that we are left at this point much as we were by St Thomas. For in treating the legal enforcement of morals, he too—albeit from a different standpoint and for other reasons—favoured a reticence on the part of the lawmaker. And his criteria for intervention are not dissimilar to the Council's: the acts of virtue which the law might prescribe are those which bear on the 'common good', the vices to be repressed are those grievously harmful without the prohibition of which society might not survive. The mention of murder and theft is perhaps enough to suggest a minimalist conception of the scope of the law's interest.

'Within Due Limits'

But what of the constraints envisaged by the Second Vatican Council? As we have seen, the 'due limits' of the exercise of the principle of freedom of religion turn out to be 'the just requirements of public order',[40] which in turn are identified later as the requirements of peace, justice and public morality, all of which are 'basic to the common good'.[41]

The expression 'common good' is a familiar one in Catholic social teaching since the time of Pope Leo XIII but its roots are in ancient Greek thought, and it is used in Christian theology from at least the time of Augustine. We have seen that Aquinas regarded it as one of the defining features of law;[42] for him it was a complex concept whose political application was only one aspect.[43] Our purposes do not require the detail which a full account of the notion would call for, and we can work with a description elsewhere provided by the Council, echoing the encyclical *Mater et Magistra* of Pope John XXIII.

The common good, according to *Dignitatis Humanae*, is 'the sum total of social conditions which allow people, either as groups or as individuals, to reach their fulfilment more fully and more easily'.[44] Even from this description it is possible to see that it is not something set over against individual good, as it were. Indeed John Finnis has remarked that the modern 'manifesto' conception of human rights is 'a way of sketching *the outlines of the common good*, the various aspects of individual well-being in community'.[45] Thus personal freedom is itself a part of the common good; and care of the common good includes the promotion of all human rights.

This is an important point because the concept is often used in public debate as though it meant something wholly separate from the freedom of individuals. Some speak of it as though it were the good of the majority or even of the State, so that the recognition of a minority or personal freedom is subject to its according with the beliefs of the majority or some objective of the State. Those who argue in this fashion appear to be untroubled by the realisation that on the logic of their position some of their own freedoms might be abridged in a society in which the majority is of a different religious or moral persuasion; nor do they seem to recognise that theirs is the logic of totalitarianism or what Maritain called state despotism.[46]

But there is more to the common good than personal freedom and individual rights, as we can see when we recall that in life in society the freedoms of the members require to be harmonised so that *each* person can flourish in the optimum measure. In this process government and law have a role, characterised in Catholic social teaching as the preservation of a 'public order'. It is easy to see why this is said to include public peace and justice; but what of 'public morality'?

8

WHOSE MORALITY, WHAT LAW?

With this question we arrive at the theme of the famous debate associated in our time with the names of Lord Devlin and H.L.A. Hart. The debate was about what is usually called the enforcement of morals and an important part of it concerned the concept of public morality. Our interest is not only in what Hart and Devlin made of that concept but also in the way in which each argued his case. For both took positions which in outline and some of their detail we may recognise as those adopted on different sides of the debates with which we have become familiar. For that reason the two sides will be set out here fairly fully and I shall draw attention to some important points.

Preliminaries

But first some preliminary clarifications. Recall that 'public morality' is usually listed as one of the bases for legal restriction of personal or group freedom. The term may for the moment be thought of as a kind of shorthand for those items of morality which commentators believe should be enforced by law. And it is the nature of its content that is in debate between Devlin and Hart and their commentators. It is usually contrasted with private morality, but the contrast often serves only to compound the problems inherent in explaining it. It is no doubt cold comfort that it is easier to say what the terms do not mean than to offer a conclusive definition. Yet it is in fact important to be able to distinguish at least some inadequate or incorrect usages.

Some think of public morality as referring to the moral beliefs of the majority in the community, or at least to those beliefs which the majority wish to see reflected in the law. In one sense this is an acceptable description: in a democratic system a statute expresses the mind and will of a parliamentary majority, itself elected by majority vote. But in debates about morality and law a false move is at this point sometimes made. For it is then concluded that if the majority of citizens are Roman Catholic (for example) there is, *by that fact and a priori*, sufficient warrant for expressing a specifically Roman Catholic belief in the law.

But this line of argument involves a confusion between two senses of 'majority', caused by a failure to distinguish between contexts. The context in which the term is used in reference to a democratic system is *political:* the parliamentary vote is the end of a process in which the political community *as such* has expressed itself. The context of the usage which refers to a Roman Catholic majority is what might be called *demographic.* The majority envisaged in the democratic principle is, of course, the political; and to equate a demographic majority with the political is, precisely, to exclude minorities from the *polis.*

The notion of private morality fares scarcely better in some of the debates. Contrasted with public morality it is invoked as designating the realm of morals which is 'not the law's business'. Perhaps the most unhelpful use of it is that which refers it merely to acts which are done in private, as though *by that fact* they are or ought to be beyond the reach of the law. Little reflection is needed to see the inadequacy of this: most murders are done in private, and privacy is virtually essential to the thief. It is of course quite a different matter to say as Lord Devlin does that 'as far as possible' privacy should be respected by the lawmaker.

Another unsatisfactory usage is that whose meaning is that a particular decision is a matter of private moral judgment, i.e. a matter upon which one is free in conscience to decide for oneself. This is unsatisfactory not because there are no acts which are matters of private judgment (it is a matter of my private judgment whether I am obliged to contribute to Trocaire's Lenten campaign), but because there are some acts which are manifestly not (morality does not allow me to make up my mind as to which troublesome acquaintance I might kill). To say that something is a matter of private judgment is usually a beginning rather than the end of an argument in debates about the enforcement of morals.

Indeed many *moral* arguments nowadays, especially in the area of personal morality, are precisely about whether a decision is purely a matter for the personal conscience judgment of an individual, unbeholden to external rule or authority, or whether there are 'objective' principles which always bind and to which personal judgment must conform. So for example the assertion that women have a right to choose abortion comes up against an assertion that direct killing of the innocent is always wrong. The point here is that whichever position is taken has to be argued for, and the argument is not settled by asserting the conclusion.

What then is public morality? In the preceding chapter we adverted to a remark by John Finnis that modern lists of human rights such as may be derived from the UN Declaration of Human Rights amount to a sketch of the outlines of the common good.[1] It might be thought that such a list can also be said to comprise or at least include a sketch of the content of public morality. We should expect states to promote and vindicate human rights, to regulate their exercise, and to punish their infraction. Why not, when considering the 'public morality' to be enforced by the law, have recourse to a typical modern list of human rights?

John Finnis offers one reason in the course of arguing for the retention of the term 'public morality' to import a qualification on the exercise of individual rights. He acknowledges that the 'logical reach' of rights talk makes it possible to say that the exercise of rights is to be limited only by respect for the rights of others. But 'human rights can only be securely enjoyed in certain sorts of milieu—a context or framework of mutual respect and trust and common understanding, an environment which is physically healthy and in which the weak can go about without fear of the whims of the strong'.[2] The fostering of an appropriate milieu is a task distinct from that of the regulation of individual rights and it deserves a separate reference. It achieves this reference in the expression 'public morality'.

Another reason why an enumeration of rights would not exhaustively describe common good is that many rights commonly listed as human rights are not specific as to their concrete content. That is—in a manner reminiscent of the formal type of principle which we encountered in an earlier chapter—they intimate a general stance or attitude toward some value or good, without saying how this attitude or stance is to be reflected in concrete terms. Take for example Article 12 of the UN Declaration which concerns marriage and the protection of family life. The terms of the Article, admirable and at a certain level crucially important though they be, do not answer the question whether a society ought to have a divorce law or not.

It would be wrong to make little of such formulations of rights on the ground that they do not always import an indisputable concrete content. It is no small gain to have even a general recognition of the value of marriage and the family, as in the Article just adverted to. And it is no small gain that nations have opted for the moral orientations signalled in the terms in which the several rights are cast. But the fact that a formulation is not specific as to content means that each society must address for itself the concrete requirements of the right which is expressed. Doubtless there is much that will be commonly agreed; but it is at this point that differences too may manifest themselves. It is at this point, in other words, that the issues comprised in the question, what is public morality? arise again.

The Wolfenden Report

The background to the Hart-Devlin debate was the publication in 1957 of the Report of the Wolfenden Committee, set up to examine existing English law concerning homosexual offences and prostitution.[3] The Committee was primarily interested in formulating proposals for the reform of the law in these areas. But it was considered useful to look for a general principle governing the enforcement of morality by law or, to put it more accurately, the legal proscription of immorality.

The Wolfenden Committee formulated this principle as follows. The function of the criminal law 'so far as it concerns the subjects of this enquiry . . . is to preserve public order and decency, to protect the citizen from what is offensive or injurious, and to provide sufficient safeguards against exploitation and corruption of others, particularly the young, weak in body and mind, inexperienced, or in a state of special physical, official or economic dependence'.[4] I shall refer to this as the Wolfenden principle although it is a version of a doctrine long linked with the name of the philosopher John Stuart Mill.[5]

An implication of the principle is then made explicit: 'It is not, in our view, the function of the law to intervene in the private lives of citizens, or to seek to enforce any particular pattern of behaviour, further than to carry out the purposes which we have outlined.'[6] One of the recommendations of the Committee accordingly was that homosexual behaviour between consenting adults in private should no longer be a criminal offence. In the context of this proposal the Report remarked that unless a deliberate attempt is to be made by society, acting through the agency of the law, to equate the sphere of crime with that of sin, 'there must remain a realm of private morality and immorality which is, in brief and crude terms, not the law's business'.[7]

Lord Devlin's View

Some two years later Sir Patrick (now Lord) Devlin subjected the Wolfenden principle to a close scrutiny in the course of a paper delivered to the British Academy.[8] Devlin interpreted the principle to mean that 'no act of immorality should be made a criminal offence unless it is accompanied by some other feature such as indecency, corruption or exploitation'.[9] It is features such as these which according to Wolfenden bring what is immoral into the public realm, and only when this happens should the law take an interest. But Devlin was uneasy with the disjunction between morals and the law which this appeared to import. He thought that it was inconsistent with existing

English law and he contended moreover that there is in fact a 'public morality' which it is the business of the law to enforce.

This contention is Lord Devlin's main thesis and he develops it in three stages. First he argues to the necessity of a public morality in the maintenance of which society has a stake. The very existence of civil society presupposes that its members share certain ideas, and these include ideas about what is right and wrong in the way in which they conduct themselves. 'If men and women try to create a society in which there is no fundamental agreement about good and evil they will fail; if, having based it on common agreement, the agreement goes, the society will disintegrate.'[10] It is for society as a whole to say what these ideas must be, and to decide what it will or will not accept by way of deviation.

But—and this is the second stage in the exposition—it is a further question whether a society should use the law to enforce its moral judgments. Should it punish deviation from accepted norms? The Wolfenden principle was that it may do so only when there is special justification for its entering the moral field: that is if immoral behaviour is also indecent, exploitative, corrupting, subversive of the public order, or otherwise socially harmful. 'If society has the right to make a judgement and has it on the basis that a recognized morality is as necessary to society as, say, a recognized government, then society may use the law to preserve morality in the same way as it uses it to safeguard anything else that is essential to its existence.'[11] Society therefore has, as Devlin puts it, a *prima facie* right to legislate against immorality 'as such'.[12]

The third stage of Lord Devlin's argument concerns the question, what items of immorality should the law forbid? And in theory, he says, there is nothing that it may not forbid. 'It is not possible to settle in advance exceptions to the general rule or to define inflexibly areas of morality into which the law is in no circumstances to be allowed to enter.'[13] Not, as he later explained, that every deviation from a society's shared morality *actually* threatens its existence, any more than does every activity that might be called subversive. But immorality and subversion in whatever form are both activities which are 'capable in their nature' of threatening the existence of society, and neither can in principle be put beyond the law.[14] In Devlin's view 'it is no more possible to define a sphere of private morality than it is to define one of private subversive activity'.[15]

In practice however the law does not attempt to forbid all immorality, and Lord Devlin goes on to examine the basis upon which it might discriminate. But first he addresses a sub-question: how are the moral judgments of society to be ascertained? There is to hand, he says,

WHOSE MORALITY, WHAT LAW?   101

a standard of judgment long familiar in English law, the standard of the
'reasonable man'. But who is he? His name notwithstanding, he is not
to be confused with the rational man. 'He is not expected to reason
about anything and his judgement may be largely a matter of feeling';[16]
and yet he is 'the right-minded man'.[17] He is the man in the street, the
man in the jury-box, the being known to the legal profession as the
man in the Clapham omnibus.[18] (Think of the man—or woman—in
Bus 66 or whatever your local service.) According to Lord Devlin
'Immorality . . . for the purpose of the law, is what every right-
minded person is presumed to consider to be immoral.'[19]

In ascertaining the content of a public's morality the legislator is
guided by the criterion which has long guided judges, the standard of
the reasonable man. But though in theory any item of that man's
morals might be made a matter of law, in practice not everything is; nor
indeed is it desirable that it should be. For the individual 'cannot be
expected to surrender to the judgement of society the whole conduct
of his life'.[20] The individual must be given some freedom, and the law
tries to balance that freedom and the public interest; and there are four
'elastic principles' which may help a legislator in pursuit of this aim.

The first is that there must be toleration of the maximum individual
freedom consistent with the integrity of society.[21] 'Nothing should be
punished by the law that does not lie beyond the limits of tolerance.'
The test is two-fold: public judgment of the practice to be prohibited
must amount to 'a real feeling of reprobation',[22] and 'there must be a
deliberate judgement that the practice is injurious to society'.[23]

The second principle which may guide a legislator is that the limits
of tolerance shift. Devlin is not here concerned with change in *moral
standards*, rather is he noting that what people are prepared to *tolerate* (as
distinct from approve) in the way of deviation may vary from time to
time. 'It follows as another good working principle that in any new
matter of morals the law should be slow to act. By the next generation
the swell of indignation may have abated and the law be left without the
backing which it needs. But it is then difficult to alter the law without
giving the impression that moral judgement is being weakened.'[24]

A third principle is that as far as possible, privacy should be respected.
Devlin notes 'a general sentiment that the right to privacy is something to
be put in the balance against the enforcement of the law',[25] and asks
whether the same should not apply in the making of law. The extent of its
application must inevitably be restricted: 'When the help of the law is
invoked by an injured citizen, privacy must be irrelevant; the individual

cannot ask that his right to privacy should be measured against injury criminally done to another.'[26] But 'when all who are involved in the deed are consenting parties and the injury is done to morals, the public interest in the moral order can be balanced against the claims of privacy'.[27]

The fourth principle which Devlin thought instructive for the legislator is that the law is concerned with minimum not maximum standards of behaviour; 'there is much in the Sermon on the Mount that would be out of place in the Ten Commandments'.[28] 'The criminal law is not a state-ment of how people ought to behave; it is a statement of what will happen to them if they do not behave; good citizens are not expected to come within reach of it or set their sights by it, and every enactment should be framed accordingly'.[29]

Devlin's position may be put summarily as follows. People who form a civil society do so on the basis of a sharing of certain ideas including moral ideas. A society's existence is threatened by deviance from the morality so shared. It is for society to say how much deviance it will tolerate, and it is entitled to use the criminal law to enforce its morality when deviance exceeds toleration's bounds. A legislator will know when this point has been reached by reference to the standard of the reasonable man.

In this view there is no private immorality in the sense envisaged by Wolfenden. The most private of acts has a social resonance, however indi-rectly produced; *any* immorality is capable in its nature of threatening a society's existence. In theory therefore there is no immoral act that might not be proscribed by law. But in practice a line must be drawn, for there should be some scope for individual freedom without injury to the public interest. And in deciding what to forbid, a lawmaker may be helped by some general principles. But there are no hard and fast rules and each case must be viewed on its merits. 'The boundary between the criminal law and the moral law is fixed by balancing in the case of each particular crime the pros and cons of legal enforcement in accordance with the sort of considerations I have been outlining.'[30]

Professor Hart's View

Lord Devlin's thesis was soon challenged by H.L.A. Hart, then Professor of Jurisprudence at Oxford.[31] Hart reviews an earlier debate between J.S. Mill and J.F. Stephen which he sees as closely paralleled in the modern exchanges.[32] He develops his own position with reference to Mill's account and he pays special attention to the arguments of Lord Devlin. Even his choice of starting-point is significant: he considers that the question whether morals should be enforced is itself a moral question. For enforcement involves the curtailment of freedom, and the curtailment of freedom requires moral justification.

Legal enforcement has two aspects. The first is the punishment of offenders, which typically consists in the deprivation of freedom of movement or of property or of association with family or friends, or the infliction of physical pain or even death. But all of these are normally regarded as evil and normally their infliction is considered wrong. If therefore it is to escape moral censure their infliction requires special justification.[33]

The second aspect of enforcement is no less pertinent to the need for justification. It is that law restricts freedom not only in the way it punishes offenders but also in that it coerces conformity through threat of punishment. Indeed, Hart says, this is what is normally in mind when people speak of the restriction of liberty by law. One's freedom is as surely even if differently inhibited when one refrains from an act for fear of being put in jail as it is when one is jailed for doing the forbidden deed. This kind of restriction also needs to be justified, for freedom is a value both in itself and because it enables people to experiment with different ways of living.[34]

But there is yet another reason, according to Hart, why restriction of freedom requires to be justified from the standpoint of morality: 'interference with individual liberty . . . is itself the infliction of a special form of suffering—often very acute—on those whose desires are frustrated by the fear of punishment'.[35] Hart observes that this is especially true of laws which impose a sexual morality.

I draw attention to Professor Hart's emphasis upon the value of freedom for it sets the tone of his entire treatment. Of course he agrees that individual freedom must sometimes be restricted in the public interest. For one thing an individual's freedom must be harmonised with the freedoms of others in the community; and it is sometimes necessary to curtail freedom so as to protect people from their own destructive impulses.[36] But he insists that there is a moral onus on whomever would abridge liberty to justify any constraint.

Hart then points to another aspect of regarding the enforcement of morals as a moral issue. 'The importance of this feature of the question is that it would plainly be no sufficient answer to show that in fact in some society—our own or others—it was widely regarded as morally quite right and proper to enforce, by legal punishment, compliance with the accepted morality . . . The existence of societies which condemn association between white and coloured persons as immoral and punish it by law still leaves our question to be argued.'[37]

It is from this vantage-point that Professor Hart elaborates his criticism of Lord Devlin's stance. First he rejects the contention that the Wolfenden principle is inconsistent with existing English law. Then, more fundamentally, he attacks Devlin's account of the 'public morality' which is necessary for the survival of society. His own position is that nothing should be outlawed solely because it is immoral but only if, also, it contravenes the principle espoused by Wolfenden and Mill, or when a particular prohibition may be warranted by 'paternalism'.[38]

But the main target of Hart's criticism is the argument which Devlin makes for the need for a public morality to be enforced through the law. Central to his objection is the belief that Devlin's account masks an undiscussed assumption: 'that all morality—sexual morality together with the morality that forbids acts injurious to others such as killing, stealing, and dishonesty—forms a single seamless web, so that those who deviate from any part of it are likely or perhaps bound to deviate from the whole'.[39]

Hart remarks that Devlin offers no evidence for this. He himself is prepared to agree that no society could exist without a morality which 'mirrored and supplemented the law's proscription of conduct injurious to others'.[40] But for him it by no means follows that *any* kind of deviation from such a code must spell disintegration for the society. And he offers an illustration: 'there is . . . no evidence to support, and much to refute, the theory that those who deviate from conventional sexual morality are in other ways hostile to society.[41]

There is an even deeper problem. To Hart's mind Devlin's view implies 'the unacceptable proposition that a society is identical with its morality as that is at any given moment of its history, so that a change in its morality is tantamount to the destruction of a society'.[42] This he finds absurd. 'Taken strictly, it would prevent us from saying that the morality of a given society had changed, and would compel us instead to say that one society had disappeared and another one had taken its place.'[43] But, Hart thinks, it is only on this 'absurd criterion' of what it is for the same society to continue to exist that it could be maintained without evidence that any deviation from a society's shared morality threatens its existence.[44]

This is an appropriate point at which to decline to follow Hart and Devlin further into the thicket of their argument. From now on the debate involves close engagement upon a variety of issues of fact and logic to do justice to which would take us beyond the ambition of this account. At one level the debate is about the adequacy of the

Wolfenden (or some similar) principle for an attempt to develop a coherent theory concerning the legal enforcement of morals. At that level the detail of the argument between Hart and Devlin and among their numerous commentators is of course crucial. At a more immediately practical level however it may be more instructive to attend to some more general features of the two positions. With this in mind it will help if we formulate again the main issues between them.

The Wolfenden principle was that no act should be prohibited by the criminal law merely because it is immoral but only if it imported additionally an identifiable social harm. Devlin thought this principle flawed and he argued that there are some acts which are rightly forbidden because they contravene the moral code. For he regarded a shared morality as pertaining to the essence of society, and deviance as a potential threat to its existence.

Hart agreed that some shared morality is necessary but he denied that every item in a society's code had a claim to be enforced by law. He particularly rejected the view that the fact that conduct is by common standards immoral is sufficient to justify making that conduct punishable. His own view is that curtailment of liberty by the law is warranted only if necessary for the prevention of harm to others or, in certain circumstances, the protection of people from their own destructive impulses.

Common Ground

The differences between the two positions are such that it is possible to lose sight of the fact that they are not without common ground. There is this much at least: that both Devlin and Hart envisage the main issue as one of reconciling individual freedom with claims of a 'common good' in some sense of that expression. Each requires advertence to a social dimension in human conduct and to a public interest in preventing social harm; and each is prepared to recognise a role for the criminal law in the process.

Indeed one commentator has remarked that they are both 'recognizably liberals',[45] meaning no doubt that each puts a premium on freedom. In Hart's case this is of course clear even in the way in which he frames the main question: is it morally permissible to enforce morality 'as such'.[46] But it is evident also in Devlin's assertion that 'the individual has a *locus standi* too; he cannot be expected to surrender to the judgement of society the whole conduct of his life'.[47] And the insight is made concrete in the 'elastic principles' to which Devlin would have the legislator advert, and especially in the requirements that there must be toleration of the maximum freedom consistent with the integrity of society and that privacy must as far as possible be respected.

Differences

On the face of it then what divides the two views is in the end a question of theory: what is the principle by which it is decided which items of immorality are to be proscribed? For Devlin the question turns upon whether or not a piece of conduct belongs to the 'public morality' in the sharing of which a society is constituted. For Hart the test is whether conduct is demonstrably injurious, to others or in certain circumstances to oneself. But perhaps more important for us than the finer points of their disagreement about ultimate theoretical principle are certain general features of the case made by each. Take first what they make of the respective claims of individual freedom and society.

We have noticed the uncompromising way in which Hart requires a moral justification of any restraint. But we saw how Devlin too wants recognition of the value of freedom. In another essay[48] he says that in speaking of a free society 'we mean no more than that we strike a balance in favour of individual freedom'. This is later amplified: 'What I mean by striking [a balance] in favour of freedom is that the question to be asked in each case is: "How much authority is necessary?" and not "How much liberty is to be conceded?"' He considers it a mark of a free society that 'authority should be a grant and liberty not a privilege'.[49]

Yet Devlin's view accords a very considerable practical priority to the moral *status quo*. In the first place he leaves us in no doubt that in speaking of public morality he means the morality to which society actually subscribes at any given time. A forceful expression of this is to be found in the Maccabean lecture. 'I have said that the morals which underly the law must be derived from the sense of right and wrong which resides in the community as a whole; it does not matter whence the community of thought comes, whether from one body of doctrine or another or from the knowledge of good and evil which no man is without. If the reasonable man believes that a practice is immoral and believes also—*no matter whether the belief is right or wrong,* so be it that it is honest and dispassionate—that no right-minded member of his society could think otherwise, then for the purpose of the law it is immoral.'[50] (my italics)

What counts for the purposes of the law therefore is society's 'positive morality' as Hart was later to call it:[51] that which is as it were laid down in the collective judgment as belonging to the community of ideas in the sharing of which a society is constituted. Moreover it is plain that for Devlin, by contrast with Hart, the onus is on whomever would escape restraint to persuade authority that the law should keep its distance. The legislator is to consult the claims of privacy and freedom but he must remember also that the limits of tolerance shift, and take care that the law move only slowly.

This bias is later defended by Devlin against the strictures of critics. Hart had accused his opponent's view of conducing to the use of legal punishment 'to freeze into immobility the morality dominant at a particular time in a society's existence'.[52] But Devlin rejects this suggestion. In fact, he points out, the law never tries to enforce the whole of public morality, and the area left uncovered is that which is most susceptible to change.[53] Even if the law were to extend to the whole 'its effect would be not to freeze but to regulate the process of liquefaction and to help distinguish the changes which are motivated by a genuine search after moral improvement from those which are relaxation into vice'.[54]

Is not this, one must nonetheless ask, to grant inordinate significance to the *status quo* and to cripple legal reform? Devlin thinks not. 'To hold that morality is a question of fact is not to deify the *status quo* or to deny the perfectibility of man. The unending search for truth goes on and so does the struggle towards the perfect society. It is our common creed that no society can be perfect unless it is a free society; and a free society is one that is created not as an end in itself but as a means of securing and advancing the bounds of freedom for the individuals who live within it.'[55] Be all of that as it may, there is a considerable burden on a legislator who before promoting a measure of the sort which is the subject of this debate is constrained *in principle* by the views of the man in the bus. I say 'in principle' because of course in practice no politician can afford to ignore the public sense. But if as a matter of principle what is estimated to be the public mind is in possession, if change in the law can *by right* come only when the lawmaker can be satisfied that the public mind has changed, the reformer is at a disadvantage indeed.

Of course this may be thought to be no bad thing; Devlin himself spoke of the value of having the time to distinguish between changes which betoken real improvement and those which are symptoms merely of a slide into vice. But not everyone will relish the notion of what might be called a principled obstacle to legal reform, as applicable to ending racial discrimination on public transport as to changing the law on divorce.

Which brings us back to the man in the bus. A second reason for unease about Lord Devlin's argument has been found by critics in his account of how the public mind is ascertained. Devlin, it will be recalled, offered several synonyms for 'the reasonable man' whose standards a lawmaker is to consult: the right-minded man, the man in the street, the man in the jury-box. He has a preference for this last, as he explains in a later paper.[56] 'When I call him the man in the jury box, I do not mean to imply that the ordinary citizen when he enters the jury box is invested with some peculiar quality that enables him to pronounce ex cathedra on morals. I still think of him simply as the ordinary reasonable man, but by placing him in the jury box I call attention to three points'.[57]

The three points are set out. 'First, the verdict of a jury must be unanimous; so a moral principle, if it is to be given the force of law, should be one which twelve men and women drawn at random from the community can be expected not only to approve but to take so seriously that they regard a breach of it as fit for punishment. Second, the man in the jury box does not give a snap judgement but returns his verdict after argument, instruction, and deliberation. Third, the jury box is a place in which the ordinary man's views on morals become directly effective. The law-maker who makes the mistake of thinking that what he has to preserve is not the health of society but a particular regimen, will find that particular laws wither away.'[58]

This makes it clear, I think, that Devlin is anxious to make terms with critics who objected to his treatment in the Maccabean lecture of the standard of the reasonable man. Their criticism was that his account virtually precluded the factor of reason in the common judgment, and opened the door to the endorsement of prejudice and all manner of irrationality. He defends himself against this charge in the Preface to *The Enforcement of Morals*,[59] perhaps not entirely persuasively. But at any rate in the later lecture he took trouble to depict 'rightmindedness' as pre-supposing a due share of 'argument, instruction and deliberation'.[60]

What of Hart's approach? It is not, as we have seen, that he sees no place for the law's proscribing immoral conduct. But it is not precisely because such conduct is in violation of a moral code that law forbids it. Rather it is that the prevention of such conduct is necessary to a society's very survival. Elsewhere he maintains that 'reflection on some very obvious generalisations—indeed truisms—concerning human nature and the world in which men live, shows that as long as these hold good, there are certain rules of conduct which any social organisation must contain if it is to be viable'.[61] The conduct proscribed by these rules is summarised in the expression 'conduct injurious to others'.

This of course is the harm-principle espoused by Mill, to which Hart is prepared to add a version of paternalism. The principle is indeed a plausible one, for no-one could sensibly dispute the desirability or the need to protect people from harm. And again there is bound to be much agreement upon what conduct is thereby precluded: the taking of life, unwarranted deprivation of freedom, injury to the person, fraudulent business transaction, damage to property, to list but some. Indeed it is fair to say that the harm-principle carries one a long distance in any discussion of what the law ought to forbid.

But the application of the principle is by no means trouble free. And one of the obvious questions to which it gives rise is as to the range of 'harm' which it contemplates. Does it refer to physical harm only—or should it be extended to cover moral harm? Does it regard harm to persons only, or has it a legitimate application to institutions—such as marriage and the family? And Professor Hart's paternalism: does that concern its object's physical good alone or should it include moral welfare? If the latter, what is there to choose between it and Lord Devlin's enforcement of morals? Such questions have been central to the modern debate; it cannot be said that they have received unequivocal answers.[62]

9

HOW IS A CATHOLIC TO VOTE?

We should now recall the exact point of interest of the Hart-Devlin debate for us. I have argued that the Catholic Church's teaching on religious freedom provides by analogy a framework within which questions of law and morality may be approached constructively. The key principle is that no-one should be made to act against his or her conscience nor restrained from acting in accordance with it 'within due limits'. This envisages a tolerance of pluralism of belief and practice in moral as in religious matters. Freedom is in possession unless its exercise is at the expense of peace, justice or public morality. And we have been exploring, through the medium of the Hart-Devlin debate, the meaning of public morality.

An implication of the exposition so far is that as regards the expression of moral value in the law the issues are the same for a Catholic as for any other citizen. And as regards the set of issues commonly summarised in the rubric 'the enforcement of morals' the central question for a Catholic is the same as it is for anyone else. The key question for everyone in any community is whether a measure which gives or witholds a particular liberty is or is not likely, all things considered, to promote the best social conditions for human flourishing.

Although there are differences of belief on what constitutes human flourishing, conscientious people of the various moral and religious traditions are likely to agree on its general lineaments. The consensus implied in the narrative of rights in, say, the UN Universal Declaration is an impressive consensus upon the central content of the common good. H.L.A. Hart's concept of a set of universal values points to a minimum content of moral and legal imperative which in substance must gain widespread agreement. Much of what Lord Devlin means by public morality is no more than is subscribed to by civilised societies everywhere.

But there are also some differences, and they affect the question of what may be enforced by the law. Even in societies whose value systems are relatively homogeneous there may be differences on the ranking of values as between one subgroup and another, or a subgroup and the majority; and there may always be differences concerning the appropriateness of various forms of legislation, or upon the question whether legislation is an appropriate response at all. The potential for difference is even more marked in communities in which there is a significant pluralism. What I have been contending is that the Catholic inheritance leaves the Catholic citizen in the same position as anyone else in coping with these differences in practice.

Hart or Devlin?

Does one opt for Hart's account or Devlin's? The point of sketching their positions here was not to argue for one rather than the other but to provide a mirror of our own discussions. And I have been suggesting that from our standpoint the most instructive differences may not be those which lie in the finer points but rather those which are intermediate in the development of their debate. In broad terms it may be said that Hart starts from a bias in favour of personal freedom whereas Devlin's touchstone, first and last, is society. It is no doubt true that, in Basil Mitchell's phrase, both are recognisably liberal; but Devlin's approach is, in an exact sense, the conservative. The point to grasp now is that neither is particularly 'Catholic'; rather are they alternative accounts which people of any moral tradition will find more or less helpful when trying to make sense of their own experience of the matters in debate.

It may indeed be, as Simon Lee has suggested, that we do not have to choose the one to the exclusion of the other. 'Hart and Devlin are painting a picture of law and morals from different vantage points. Both can deepen our understanding of law and morals. Both reveal something of their own vantage point from the picture which they paint.'[1] At any rate neither account relieves the civic community or its government from thinking through in every case which values it wishes to have promoted by the law and how. And the argument is seldom clear-cut.

Guidelines

But are there any guidelines? Someone, legislator or citizen, faced with a vote on a measure of the sort in question here will not be much consoled to learn that neither Hart nor Devlin nor any of their commentators has found the key to all the problems. I suggest however that the debate has not left us without some practical guidelines.

There are, for example Devlin's 'elastic principles': a bias towards freedom and privacy, a caution about changing fashions of thought and value, a sense of modesty about what law can do. Those who favour Hart's approach may be helped by questions suggested by Simon Lee:

1. What is the harm (from which there is question of giving legal protection)?
2. Who or what is harmed?
3. How serious is the harm?
4. Are there countervailing benefits?
5. Do those harmed need or deserve society's protection?
6. What level of protection is most appropriate, bearing in mind the costs or disadvantages?[2]

Another kind of criterion was proposed by John Courtney Murray: 'A legal ban on evil must consider what St. Thomas calls its own "possibility". That is, will the ban be obeyed, at least by the generality? Is it enforceable against the disobedient? Is it prudent to undertake the enforcement of this or that ban, in view of the possibility of harmful effects in other areas of social life? Is the instrumentality of coercive law a good means for the eradication of this or that social vice? And, since a means is not a good means if it fails to work in most cases, what are the lessons of experience in the matter? What is the prudent view of results—the long view or the short view?'[3]

Murray's questions have their origin in a sense of the differences between morality and law, and in the pragmatism which must attend a realistic politics. An underlying theme is that of community consent: in the absence of backing by the people 'law either withers away or becomes tyrannical'.[4] This is true of every community but in a religiously pluralist society it may be crucial: 'Basic religious divisions lead to conflict of moral views; certain asserted "rights" clash with other "rights" no less strongly asserted. And the divergences are often irreducible'.[5] Hence Murray believed that the public consensus must include agreement on rules to regulate the interrelationships of the divergent groups, as well as their common relation to the order of law.[6]

Murray proposed four such rules; he was speaking about censorship in the arts and literature, but Richard McBrien has suggested that the rules have a more general application and has re-stated them accordingly: 'First, . . . each group retains the right to demand conformity from its own members . . . Secondly, no group in a pluralist society has the right to expect that government will impose or prohibit some act of behaviour when there is no support for such action in society at large. Thirdly, any group has the right to work towards a change in moral standards within the pluralist society, through the use of methods of persuasion and pacific argument. Fourthly, no group has the right to impose its own religious or views on others, through the use of methods of force, coercion or violence.[7]

Presupposed in these rules are, in Murray's words, 'the jurisprudential proposition that what is commonly imposed by law on all our citizens must be supported by general public opinion, by a reasonable consensus of the whole community'.[8] This raises again a question touched on earlier: since in a democratic society law is the outcome of majority decision is it not a matter of simple logic that majority values will be enshrined in the law? And where a majority of citizens happen to be of a particular moral tradition can anyone complain if it is that tradition's positions which are so enshrined?

Attention has already been drawn to the risk of confusing the concepts of the demographic and the political: a political majority is achieved in course of all that is comprised in the notion of the democratic process, and at the level of theory it cannot be said to be determined in advance by adherence to a religious or cultural majority. Legislation involving the enforcement of morals is the product of a process of debate upon the measure, including upon the question whether in this case the claim of some minority interest is to be catered for. A consensus thus reached is not reflective only of the belief which the majority holds about the substantive morality of the subject matter of the proposed legislation; for it includes also a judgment on the legislation's aptness, in the form proposed, and with regard to all the circumstances of its enactment here and now.

Creating A Consensus

Meanwhile it is of course open to any person or group to seek to influence the consensus. I shall later comment on some of the special problems which this may bring when the influence comes from the corporate or institutional Church, especially when that Church has the allegiance of the majority of citizens. But two general points seem worth making now.

The first is in regard to attitudes to special interest groups who seek to influence the public mind with the aim of changing public policy. An 'establishment' is perhaps bound to regard as a nuisance groups which try to change the status quo; the establishment's irritation will be in proportion to its interest in keeping things the way they are. It is salutary to think that much social legislation which we now accept as admirable had its origins in the endeavours of minority interests: one need go no further than to mention labour law, laws promoting equality for women, and the first stirrings of a sense of responsibility for the environment. Ladislas Örsy has written that 'in a healthy social body the emergence of special interest groups is not a sickness, is not an aberration, is not even a nuisance, but it is a manisfestation of life. Without the ongoing pressure of special interest groups, the common good could become atrophied, stale and static, and be reduced to a kind of deadly formality'.[9]

Of course, as Örsy also says, the pursuit of a special interest has value and meaning only in the context of the common good.[10] And this will be the precise area of debate in any given issue. The practical resolution of the debate lies in the processes of democratic politics. 'On the practical level of political action, the natural conflict between the demands of the common good and the postulates of special interest groups will be resolved through the operation of the traditional structures of our own democracy as we know it. There, often enough, the ideal which can be determined abstractly cannot be obtained concretely. Therefore a compromise must be made. A need for compromise can be and indeed often is, part of the common good. It is not a denial of the ideal but its adaptation to the real.'[11]

My second point concerns the possibility of using legislation in creating a consensus. In the US debate about the duties of the office-holder, some politicians invoked the absence of consensus as a factor in their judgment that it was not feasible to seek to translate their moral beliefs about abortion into law. But, as Cardinal Bernardin has remarked, 'the fact that a spontaneous public consensus is lacking at a given moment does not prohibit its being created. When he was told that the law could not legislate morality, Dr. Martin Luther King, Jr. used to say that the law could not make people love their neighbors but it could stop their lynching them. Law and public policy can also be instruments of shaping a public consensus; they are not simply the product of consensus.'[12]

This is consistent with the concept of law as educative. It is also, incidentally, implied in the notion that legislators should be open to the claims advanced by special interest groups who may be the bearers of fresh insight into the common good. It is of course not without danger for, used crudely, it could amount to a coercion which is harsh and degrading and in the end counterproductive.

It is arguable that the use of the law in shaping consensus is more appropriate to some issues than to others. One might perhaps say that when a measure affects in the first place an *institution* rather than personal life it is more apt for use in the forging of consensus. Take the case of capital punishment: its abolition is the abolition of an institution, and it is on the institution of government that pressure is brought in order to secure that end. It is therefore in a sense an impersonal issue, except of course for those whose lives are spared if it is abolished, and perhaps for some who feel distress at the removal of what they believe to be a curb on threats to life. Something comparable is true of laws to end discrimination: their impact is first and primarily on institutions which embody discriminatory states of affairs.

Other issues however are more directly personal in their resonance. The availability or otherwise of abortion, for example, is a matter which reaches directly into the personal life of individual women. If law is brought into play in the absence of consensus it is experienced as a direct invasion of the realm of the personal, unprepared for by what Murray called persuasion and pacific argument. One can understand how a politician might consider that the law's bluntness makes it less apt for the task of helping build consensus in that case.[13]

I am not of course arguing against legal restriction of abortion *per se*, nor do I mean to question the commonly-made suggestion that there exists already in the US a consensus against abortion on demand. All I wish to do is to illustrate the point that the use of the law in creating a consensus may be more (or less) suited to some issues than to others. I shall return later to the question of the right way to try to create consensus as regards such issues as abortion.

Candidates for public office and their parties usually have characteristic programmes or 'platforms', partly derived from their ideology or political philosophy, partly shaped by the preoccupations of the hour and the place. The programmes may involve a ranking of issues, again sometimes on a philosophical or ideological basis, sometimes as a matter of pragmatic option. In some circumstances this may mean a relative inattention to an item which in a given citizen's moral code may loom large. Such—at the risk of overusing the example—is the case with abortion in the politics of the United States at the present time.

It is sometimes asked whether there is a casuistry, a method of approach to the individual issues of a political programme, which would enable a Catholic citizen to discriminate as to which programme or candidate is morally preferable. If this means a kind of Catholic calculus or ready-reckoner which would help sort candidates out on the basis of their positions on matters of Catholic morality, it is an aspect of the thesis of this book that there is no such thing. Even if a hierarchy of moral values could be agreed it is a further question, as we have repeatedly seen, how the ranking might affect the formation of public policy and the making of specific law.

J. Bryan Hehir acknowledges a theoretical possibility of ranking the items of the Catholic moral credo. But then he asks whether this means that such a hierarchy can or should be transposed to the public policy arena. 'It does not seem that such a move is either obligatory or even advisable. The direct illation from a statement of moral theory to public policy would inevitably fail to address precisely those issues which are the central factors in the wise shaping of public policy.'[14] What these factors are, says Hehir, were indicated by John Courtney Murray in the course of a critique of an exclusively personal conception of moral theory: 'It did not understand the special moral problems raised by the institutionalisation of human action. It did not grasp the nature of politics, the due autonomy of the political, the limiting factors of political action or the standing of success as a political value'.[15]

In all of the foregoing it is not at all suggested that the standpoint of the legislator is somehow amoral; the concept of the common good is a moral concept. Rather it is that the standpoint of the legislator—or of the citizen in regard to legislation—is not that of purely personal moral agency. It is not that politics and legislation are unconcerned with morality; rather it is that the concern is at a different level than that at which one lives out a personal morality through personal moral decision. And the judgment which it involves is more complex. The materials of the lawmaker's art, or many of them, are materials also of personal or interpersonal morality. But the shape which the lawmaker gives them is different, for he/she must see them from a different point of view.

Personal Conscience and Public Office
It is on this basis that it has become usual for Catholic politicians to distinguish between the requirements of personal moral conviction and their duties as office-holders or as seekers of office. This was the response of John F. Kennedy faced with the task of persuading a suspicious electorate that a Catholic president would not attempt to abridge the religious liberty guaranteed under the First Amendment of the Constitution. Commonly regarded as an expression of the so-called 'Courtney Murray doctrine',[16] (later to be the basis of the Vatican Council's Declaration on Religious Freedom), this seemed to be an acceptable account of a Catholic politician's responsibilities until called in question during the US presidential election campaign of 1984.

To understand what happened it is necessary to recall that in 1973 the United States suddenly found themselves with abortion laws which were among the most liberal in the world. For the Supreme Court judged that the legislation operative in the different states—the exact scope of which varied from state to state—was unconstitutional in depriving women of a right to choose abortion as a way of coping with unwanted pregnancy.[17] The effect of the judgment was that existing state legislation was struck down; and the enacting of restrictive legislation subsequently has been inhibited by the fear of unconstitutionality.

Since then the Catholic bishops have been at the forefront of a counter-movement which has campaigned for more restrictive laws in the name of the right to life of the foetus. This is no cause for surprise in view of Catholic Church teaching concerning the sacredness of life from the moment of conception. But inevitably it was a matter of special interest in relation to the candidature of Geraldine Ferraro, a Catholic, as Democratic candidate for the vice-presidency in 1984. Ms Ferraro's reply to journalists' questions about her position on abortion was to invoke a distinction between personal moral (she called it religious) belief and her 'standing on the issues'.

There followed some exchanges between Ms Ferraro and Archbishop John O'Connor of New York, who had already been voicing dissatisfaction with the type of response which the candidate was now making. The O'Connor-Ferraro exchanges themselves shed little light upon the question of the separability of private conscience and public responsibility *per se*, for as they developed they became concerned with Ms Ferraro's account of Catholic teaching concerning the *morality* of abortion, and with the responsibility of a Catholic office-holder in relation to public funding of abortion. But they gave impetus to a debate which had begun some months earlier and whose reverberations are still felt in the United States.[18]

I have said that Archbishop O'Connor had already intimated a dissatisfaction with the type of response which Ms Ferraro was to make—at least if, as he saw it, it amounted in practice to condoning a pro-choice view. Indeed he had opined that a Catholic could not in good faith vote for a pro-choice candidate. And New York's Governor Mario Cuomo, also a Catholic, had taken issue with him on this point directly, saying that for himself, while he agreed with the Archbishop on the morality of abortion, he must as an office-holder respect the law; nor could he see a realistic prospect for a constitutional amendment which would lead to a ban on abortion.

The debate between O'Connor and Cuomo was given new interest and renewed impetus by the episode involving Ferraro. Soon the main protagonists were joined by other prominent representatives of religious and political interests in the United States. An election atmosphere was not conducive to clarity or objectivity and it proved extremely difficult to debate principles of political philosophy or of moral theology without appearing politically partisan.

Discussion of the issues outlasted the 1984 campaign of course; nor has the last word yet been said. A review of the main contributions would be instructive, especially since the relative simplicities of the earlier stages have long given place to careful and sophisticated analysis and constructive commentary. But the US debate has been extensively and intensively canvassed elsewhere;[19] and perhaps there is merit in attempting a reflection upon the issues in abstraction from that debate's specifics.

A Principled Compromise?

The central question, once again, is that of the relationship between a politician's personal moral beliefs and his/ her responsibility in regard to policy in the public domain. This question arises most obviously when an office-holder is faced with public decisions which run counter to the moral values by which that person is guided in private life. But of course it may arise also by anticipation, for example in an election campaign, as it did for Geraldine Ferraro. And, at one remove but no less pointedly, it may arise for any citizen when it comes to voting for a candidate in the circumstances in which Ms Ferraro found herself.

We may for simplicity's sake focus on the case of the office-holder, actual or potential; and it may help if we choose an issue of the same order as abortion but somehat less controversial. Although the issues are by no means identical and there are strict limits to the comparison, capital punishment is comparable to abortion in that it concerns the taking of life. Suppose then that I am opposed to capital punishment, believing it to be an unjustified taking of life. Am I, a politician, morally obliged to campaign to have it abolished?

At first it must seem that if I believe capital punishment to be wrong I will surely want to have it abolished, and I shall be asking how I might use my power to help this end, rather than interrogating myself upon the existence of an obligation to do so. But even if I consider myself obliged to work for the abolition of the death penalty I have not yet faced the question what, concretely, am I obliged to do?

It would be manifestly ludicrous to hold that morality requires that I should never have anything to do with a system or party which condones behaviour of which I personally disapprove. If this were the only option, who with rudimentary integrity could engage in the business of politics? And how, apart from revolution, could there be any change? In any case we saw that the law's purposes sometimes prescribe tolerance even of conduct whose wrongness is universally agreed.

It can no doubt be pointed out that there is a difference between condoning and promoting, and that a separate problem arises for an office-holder faced with a measure which amounts to the active support or promotion of what he or she regards as wrongdoing. What of public funding of condoms as part of an AIDS campaign? What of a legislator, personally opposed on moral grounds to the use of artificial contraceptives in any case, who is called on to vote funding for the free supply of contraceptives by a health authority? What of budgetary provision for the institution of capital punishment? What of funding for abortion?

In standard Catholic moral theology a way of dealing with this type of question is to regard it as an issue of 'cooperation in the sin of another'.[20] The starting-point of this approach is that if something is morally wrong one ought to keep as far away from it as possible. But circumstances may make total distancing impractical—or even in some sense undesirable— and the measure of what might be called morally plausible cooperation is found through the application of certain principles and rules of thumb.

First, a distinction is made between immediate and mediate cooperation. The former involves a collaboration in the evil act itself, as when someone actively assists a thief in taking another's property. Cooperation is mediate when the cooperator provides some means necessary to a principal agent's achievement of his or her purpose; supplying a gun to a murderer is an example. Mediate cooperation is further classified as proximate or remote, depending upon the closeness of its connection to the action of the main agent. An accomplice who hands a gun to a killer is engaging in proximate cooperation; the cooperation of whoever sold him the gun is obviously more remote.

A second level of distinction is made between formal and material cooperation, referring respectively to cooperation which amounts to a deliberate personal endorsement of the immorality in question and cooperation which does not. In Catholic theology a sin is committed when one deliberately does what one knows to be wrong. Formal cooperation in the sin of another would require one's collaboration in the action knowing that it was wrong but *knowing also that the other knew it was wrong and yet chose freely to perform it*. Formal cooperation at any level is, for obvious reasons, considered as objectionable as the immorality itself and so never justified. Immediate cooperation too is precluded; it is too closely bound up with the achievement of the evil result to admit of any real moral distancing on the part of the collaborator.

Material cooperation is so called because one's actions are the 'material' of a sharing of the main action (or omission or state of affairs). It differs from formal cooperation in that it does not involve a personal endorsement of what is being done; it bespeaks an engagement which is more or less reluctant on the part of the cooperator. This kind of cooperation is evaluated partly in terms of its 'proximity' or 'remoteness' to the main action, partly in terms of the character of the reason which makes one consider cooperating at all. Proximity and remoteness are not of course merely physical; these terms refer rather to the relationship between the cooperator's contribution and the main agent's achievement.

We have seen that immediate cooperation cannot be justified; but proximate or remote material cooperation might be justifiable by a 'proportionate reason'. The exclusion of immediate cooperation is largely a matter of common sense: the more closely one is involved in an action the more difficult it is to avoid 'formal' engagement; and of course an outside observer must find it impossible to distinguish. Of course if cooperation of any kind is to make moral sense there must be a reason for it; and so it is said that even remote cooperation will not be defensible unless there is a 'proportionate' reason.

Speaking broadly one might say that this implies that one's reasons must have a certain weight and that the closer one comes to the main action the weightier one's reasons must be. The concept of a proportionate reason is a technical one in moral theology however, and it happens to be at the centre of another current debate among moralists, the debate about moral absolutes. The debate does not question the validity of the concept of proportionate reason but only the range of its application. Without entering the debate therefore we may avail ourselves of an account of the concept which the debate has provided and which will help a more precise use of it here.

Recall again that we are considering the status of behaviour which in greater or lesser degree amounts to a cooperation in what we believe to be wrongdoing. We are considering, that is, actions or omissions which are as it were tainted by their connection with what we hold to be wrong. Standard Catholic moral theology, while precluding formal cooperation and immediate material cooperation as explained above, concedes that mediate material cooperation, proximate or remote, may be justified by a proportionate reason. And in a valuable contribution to the discussion mentioned above,[21] Richard McCormick has suggested that the presence or absence of proportionality may be gauged by reference to three tests. First, he says, a value at least equal to the value being sacrificed must be at stake. Second, there must be no other way of protecting the value here and now. Third, the manner of its protection here and now must not be such as would undermine it.

So a legislator contemplating a policy or measure which had the effect of assisting or promoting immorality would have to consider first the 'proximity' of the contribution to the wrong in question. Then must come the question whether the contribution might nevertheless be warranted in virtue of a 'proportionate reason'. And this might be looked at from either of two points of view: for the legislator might consider *either* the morality of abstaining or resigning, *or* the morality of going along with what is being proposed.

He or she would be asking therefore what all the values at issue in the decision were. And how should these be best served, one way or another, now? Is there no other way of realising the values being sought? Or is there a danger that what I propose to do now, though it secures these values for the present, carries within it the possibility of undermining them in the long or the short run?

To return to the case of capital punishment, and supposing I am voting upon a budget which makes provision, explicit or implicit, for the funding of personnel and equipment in its regard: am I entitled to vote in favour, or am I bound to abstain or resign? What if my abstention would bring the government down, or otherwise injure its plan for the promotion of what it conceives to be the common good? Or what if opposition must sooner or later cost me my seat in the legislature?

In the balance is continued cooperation in an institution which I believe to be immoral, with the good (including perhaps the abolition of capital punishment) which I may hope to achieve by staying in office, or which I may hope from my party's continuing to govern. And suppose there is no other way in which the values which I seek may be safeguarded. McCormick would nevertheless require us to look at what I am doing so as to ascertain that it is not the kind of thing which on its own logic would damage these values. In the example of capital punishment, and supposing I am inclined to go along with the budget, I should be asking whether my vote implies any actual or future threat to the values I wish to preserve.

Could abstention or resignation or other disengagement be a matter of obligation ever? Of course the answer must be yes. It could be that in a particular case one's private conscience is so compromised in a public role that the only honourable resolution lies in renunciation of the role. Such a decision is obviously both personal and particular, and the judgment as to when it may be called for is in the end for the conscience of the individual concerned. There is no need to elaborate upon the perils of subjectivism and self-delusion; it is only common sense that someone in such case will take advice. An outsider can help keep objective aspects in view, including the claims of moral principle. But it is for the person concerned to make the final judgment.

Some may find uncongenial the kind of analysis which is involved in the application of the traditional approach to cooperation or in McCormick's tests. One kind of mind will find it imprecise; where do you draw the line as between proximate and remote? Another will consider it fussy, making ado about what is no more than an exercise in common sense. Yet another will be unsympathetic to its distinction-making or its casuistry. I do not wish to pretend that it will turn up neat answers nor reduce the complexity of concrete decision; and no-one would want it to be used in aid of a moral sophistry. But this analysis or something like it, deployed in a manner which is not merely mechanical or legalistic, can offer a way in to the moral complexity of some kinds of political decision. In particular it can help us attend to all morally relevant factors, avoiding either a crude application of abstract principle or the collapse of principle under the weight of the situation.

Some authors[22] have observed that the standard textbook account of cooperation was developed in a period in which the most that was likely to be said in favour of the perpetrator of what Catholic teaching considered wrong was that he/she might be excused owing to invincible ignorance. And, they point out, this does not take account of the right to freedom of conscience acknowledged in *Dignitatis Humanae*, on the basis of which a much more positive evaluation of the other person's belief is possible. This is a most important consideration, the force of which I do not wish to deny in the slightest here. Yet even if the point were not granted the standard principles on cooperation might still be applied. The cooperation envisaged in our discussion is with people who are, *ex hypothesi*, engaged in actions which Catholic teaching regards as wrong, and that is the hypothesis which is addressed by the standard account. My own point is simply that even the standard account will support some compromise in complex situations of the kind in contemplation here.

What to Do? Who is to Judge?

Our discussion up to now has been from the point of view of what is morally tolerable by way of acquiescence in or endorsement of a measure or policy which is not consistent with one's personal moral beliefs. Its import is that, on standard principles concerning cooperation in sin, there is room for compromise. But one who compromises upon a matter of personal conviction will naturally be uneasy and will have a mind to work to change the situation. I may approve the budget which provides for capital punishment, but if I am serious in my belief that it is wrong I shall continue to want its abolition.

What am I to do? The answer can only be that I must do what in my conscientious judgment is possible. And what is possible in politics is dependent upon a great variety of factors, and in the first place the achievement of office itself. But this presents a problem; for it may be plain that to make capital punishment a campaign issue will assuredly lead to my defeat. So I shall be disposed not to make too much of it, and to hope that my opponent won't. And should it come up, I shall want to reassure the voters that, great as my desire for change is, I do not wish to force my point of view. But I cannot be at ease. If I believe that each execution is a wrongful taking of a human life I cannot rest content in an ethos in which it is accepted. I shall be glad of groups who campaign for change. I shall want church leaders to speak out. I shall myself do all I can to help build a consensus.

But only I can judge what I must do. The experienced practitioner it is who knows what it takes to be elected, to bring about a change in party policy, to get the legislature to pass a law. He or she can make a mistake; nor is the politician any the less liable to laziness or apathy or failure of moral courage than the rest. No system, no party, no person is immune from criticism, including criticism from a moral point of view. An outsider may question the wisdom, including the moral wisdom, of a decision; may even wonder about the *bona fides* of the decider— though who can judge the heart? Yet it is with each politician's conscience that the judgment ultimately lies: what now, practically, must be done in service of the common good?

Politicians who invoke a distinction between personal moral belief and their responsibilities as public officials are making a distinction which is valid. It is not that there are two moralities, or that immorality may be perpetrated in a public cause. Rather is it that the judgment as to what is morally feasible in the public arena, and especially as regards legislation, is more complex than in private. There are some items of a personal moral credo which are not apt for legislation; a law against lying would not get very far. There are others about which it is possible to debate the best legislative course: should there be an absolute ban on pornography? Yet others are not sufficiently widely shared to warrant a law which would restrict those who don't hold them as well as those who do. And these are only some of the factors which complicate a legislator's task.

So the distinction is valid. But it ought not to be used as a cover for indifference to morality in the public realm. Public policy judgments are complex but they are not amoral. There is a moral obligation to promote the common good. And if I believe in the desirability of a measure, from a moral as from any other viewpoint, I shall want to see it carried through. It would make no sense to consider myself as an office-holder discharged from all practical responsibility to what is in fact a matter of my conviction. But it is I in the end who must judge what practically must be done.

If this line of reasoning is sound it is difficult to fault the response of Governor Cuomo and other US politicians who are Catholic and who yet claim the freedom to make up their own minds upon the question of abortion legislation and the concomitant issue of the provision of public funding for abortion. By the same token it is difficult to follow the arguments of those churchmen who appear to rule out 'compromise' altogether.

It is of course right to insist that there cannot be a discontinuity between personal moral conviction and public responsibility. But there remains the question, how is the connection to be expressed in political practice? And that is a question for the art and conscience of the politician. It may be that in the statements of prelates such as Cardinal O'Connor what we have is a pastoral response to the situation as they assess it. It may be, that is, that they are concerned lest a facile invocation of the distinction between personal conscience and the judgment appropriate to public office lead to a dilution of central convictions of the Catholic tradition concerning abortion. And no doubt they have every reason to fear for the purity of that tradition in present conditions in the United States. An outsider may not presume to assess their pastoral assessment. Yet one must also say that no pastoral exigency can abrogate the principle that the art of lawmaking is the legislator's proper art.

10

THE CHURCH, THE
MARKETPLACE AND THE FORUM

The focus of this book was the question, how is a Catholic expected to vote on issues which involve the embodiment of moral beliefs in law? Although an attempt was made to keep an eye to broader aspects the question has been considered with particular reference to issues usually addressed under the rubric 'the enforcement of morals'. It is freely conceded that our question is only one of those which may arise concerning the bearing of Christian faith on life in political society.[1] Yet it is a focal question, for to participate in the democratic process as citizen or politician is to engage in the work of shaping the conditions of life in society. And the casting of a vote in the legislature or at the hustings is a strongly concrete expression of one's mind as to what those conditions should be.

The main contention was that when issues like this fall to be decided Catholics are in principle in the same case as is anyone else. For the fundamental project is the reconciliation of individual freedoms with the claims of a common good, and this is a requirement of social living even if all the religions were to wither away. The Catholic theological inheritance leaves us with a principle which, if I have argued correctly, may be extended to say that in moral as in religious matters people should be free to follow their lights within the requirements of a common good. And a signal mark of this freedom is immunity from coercion by the law.

But what in service of the common good should the law forbid or enjoin? Again there is no 'Catholic answer'; or rather the Catholic's answer, like that of the neighbour not of the faith, is forged in the complex experience of social life in the polis today. We saw some of the ways in which an attempt may be made to make sense of that experience, in general theoretical terms or more practically. It will have been obvious that there is no escaping a patient engagement with each issue in its own time and place.

The impossibility of easy resolutions, theoretical or practical, will surprise no-one who reflects for a while on the moral life or the political.

But the book's argument may have bred a different kind of unease. For—to simplify—it has stressed the Catholic's freedom in the political arena; and this might arouse suspicion from two quite different standpoints.

Two Sceptics

The first standpoint is that of a believer who might feel that the approach here adopted does not make enough of the values of the Christian way. I am not thinking of the integrist for whom the Church's mission is a kind of imperialism of the soul, but rather of someone who is conscious in the first place of the Christian faith's 'demands' and who fears instinctively their dilution. The second standpoint is that of the critic, also conscious of the faith's demands, and not at all persuaded that, for all that has been argued here, the fundamental ambition of the Church or Churches is not to enforce those demands on unbeliever and believer alike.

Perhaps one ought only to say of any reader who has taken either of these impressions, that for them the argument of the book has failed. Yet it might be useful by way of conclusion to regard such hypothetical reactions as inviting clarification of some issues which lie beneath the surface of the exposition. For it is the case that the Catholic Church understands itself to have a social mission, informed by a moral vision which is not at all unspecific. Must it not feel impelled to fulfil its mission, to implement its vision? And will not this sense of mission sooner or later involve it in an encroachment on the consciences of people other than its own?

In *Centesimus Annus* Pope John Paul II wrote that 'to teach and to spread her social doctrine pertains to the Church's evangelizing mission and is an essential part of the Christian message, since this doctrine points out the direct consequences of that message in the life of society and situates daily work and struggles for justice in the context of bearing witness to Christ the Saviour'.[2] This is but the most recent statement of a theme familiar now in Catholic thought. A particularly memorable expression of it emerged from the 1971 Synod of Bishops when they spoke of 'action on behalf of justice and participation in the transformation of the world' as 'a constitutive dimension of the preaching of the Gospel'.[3]

Our review of the biblical data has shown the scriptural under-pinning; recall again Luke's portrayal of Jesus in the synagogue presenting himself as the fulfilment of Isaiah's word: 'The Spirit of the Lord is upon me, because he has anointed me to preach good news to the poor. He has sent me to proclaim release to the captives and recovering of sight to the blind, to set at liberty those who are oppressed, to proclaim the acceptable year of the Lord.'[4]

So both the believer and the critic are right to insist that the the gospel impels to action in the world. And each is also right to insist that the Church has a vision for humankind by which this action is inspired and shaped; and that the vision bespeaks commitment to quite specific values. Whoever professes to be Christian thereby *undertakes* to respect human life, to work for justice, to seek for peace, to do the truth in love (Eph. 4: 15). And the undertaking is made concrete, formulated in such specific guides for action as that a just wage is the right of a worker; or that sexual intercourse belongs to the kind of committed relationship which societies know as marriage; or that it is wrong directly to take innocent life.

David Hollenbach has written that '[t]hough Christian faith is an eminently personal act that relates the believer to God, it is never the act of an individual apart from the Church as a community of faith. Thus it is evident that the Christian vocation to work for greater justice and peace in society must be a communal undertaking'.[5] Christian values issue in action in the personal lives of believers, in the manifold contexts in which these lives are lived. But the believer is one of a community, and faith is expressed too in specifically community action. The Christian faith permeates the world not just as it is lived personally by the faithful but also through the presence in and to the world of, in Hollenbach's terminology, the Church as a corporate community.[6]

This is the point at which our critic's deepest fear is activated. For what can this mean but that the Church through its leadership and other institutions must involve itself in the public arena? And what can *that* mean but an intrusion into the lives of people who do not share the Church's faith? It is at this point that our critic invokes the principle of separation of Church and State, in the hope perhaps of driving the Church out of the public arena or at least of countering its impact.

It is of course impossible to drive the Church out in any country where freedom of religious belief and practice is guaranteed by the constitution or by law. For it is of the essence of the right thus guaranteed that the religions are at liberty to enter the marketplace and propose their doctrines and try to persuade people of their truth. The principle of the separation of Church and State, as is often said, is meant to ensure not just that no particular religion is favoured but also that none is denied room for its exercise and promotion within the law. The Vatican

Council's Declaration, of which crucial use has been made in the argument of this book, states that it is an implication of the principle of religious freedom that religious communities have the right 'not to be prevented from freely demonstrating the special value of their teaching for the organisation of society and the inspiration of all human activity'.[7]

Our anxious believer may therefore be assured both of the Church's continuing commitment to the values of the Gospel and of its intent to claim the space offered it by state guarantees of religious belief and practice wherever these exist. But the critic is likely to be the more fearful for this reminder; and both believer and critic may, from their different standpoints, persist in their unease concerning the manner of the Church's impact in the public arena in today's world.

The critic pictured here is extremist, counterpart of the fundamentalist in religion; only a minority will want to silence the Churches or put them out of the public arena altogether. But the kind of reserve about the manner of Church engagement with 'the world', of which this critic is an extreme exponent, is to be found even among people sympathetic to religion's claims and the Churches' social role. A Church which wishes to be faithful to its mission must seek to decipher the rationale of this reserve and learn from it.

Some reserve is rooted in prior theological questions. Should the 'corporate Church' confine itself to negative critique: the Church and our world are not the kingdom of God, and their ways stand permanently under the judgment of kingdom values, always falling short and therefore never to be absolutised?[8] Or should a more constructive contribution be attempted: engagement in the world's struggles, speaking to its concerns, participating in its transformation?[9] Or is 'openness' the enemy of 'faithfulness', 'dialogue' at odds with 'prophecy'?

And there are other questions. Granted a constructive involvement, what are its limits? Should hierarchy promote a Christian vision for humanity, leaving the specifics to be worked out in the experience of laity and with due regard to the autonomy of secular pursuits? Or is there a place for concrete *magisterium,* and what might be its terms and the conditions of its effective exercise? Is there a place for 'corporate' involvement of the Church?

This book, both explicitly and by implication, has contended for all that is comprised in the notion of engagement in and with the world which the Church inhabits. This is, I think, the substance of the Catholic Christian way, and its main modern expression and reference point is the doctrine of the Second Vatican Council. I hope I have not appeared to overlook the force of other views, nor to have given a false impression concerning the problems of theory or practice to which the views here espoused give rise.

But at this point perhaps we might assume a Church which inhabits a wider society and is engaged with it, and turn our attention to some of the conditions of an effective engagement in the world of today. In doing so I shall have in mind a second type of reserve about Church involvement in the arena of public business: that of our hypothetical critic haunted by the spectre of a tyranny of religion or morals; but also that of the less unsympathetic observer, even the believer, who is uneasy not so much about the principle of Church engagement in the secular realm as about aspects of the manner in which the engagement may take place.

David Hollenbach has put his finger on a key problem: 'The legitimate authority of the political arena, expressed in the principles of religious liberty and separation of Church and State,[10] raises serious questions about the possibility of common Christian action for justice. If common action is to be effective in a bureaucratic society it must be organised action. There is a strong cultural bias present in our society that results in the misinterpretation of any public or political activity by the Church as a violation of the separation of Church and State.' Hollenbach was writing of the United States but his words have more general application, including to Irish society.

The roots of this bias are complex: some lie in the particular history of a local Church or nation—the pluralist circumstances of the founding of the United States for example; others are in cultural and philosophical developments formative of modern western society; still others in some less admirable aspects of the demeanour of the Churches in the past. It avails little for Churchmen to console themselves by simplicities about the secularism of the age. Nor is the bias to be evaluated wholly negatively.

For it is associated in part with traits of the modern mind whose worth is acknowledged in the official doctrine of the Catholic Church now. ' Contemporary man is becoming increasingly conscious of the dignity of the human person, more and more people are demanding that men should exercise fully their own judgment and a responsible freedom in their actions and should not be subject to the pressure of coercion but be inspired by a sense of duty.' The Council searches the Christian heritage for evidence of the consonance of these aspirations with truth and justice.[11]

At any rate the bias of which David Hollenbach speaks, however evaluated, is a factor in the work of evangelisation. If Church presence in the public realm is perceived as threatening, that is a problem for the Churches. And it is especially a problem for Church leadership, for it is primarily in the institutions of their leaderships that the Churches as corporate entities express themselves in the public domain. It is for the leaderships especially to identify the fears to which this expression may give rise and to seek to meet them in fidelity to their gospel mission. The fears vary from place to place and indeed from time to time. But perhaps one might list some common or recurrent ones in reference to Catholicism. I shall put them in extreme form here but even when not found extremely, versions of them, or their residue, affect perception of the Church's presence and intent.

The classical fear is that of 'Rome rule': the notion that for Catholics, politics as well as doctrine are subject to Vatican diktat. Fear of Rome rule bedevilled a phase of Irish history and it is still invoked in the tortured modern politics of the North. There is a fear too of the reach of Roman Catholic *magisterium.* The claim to teach author-itatively on morals as well as faith is thought to seek a warrant to enter boardroom and bedroom, marketplace and forum. In an ethos which is individualist and liberal, resistance to a claim thus perceived is instinctive and deep. A third fear is of 'clericalism': fear of a society in which power is held by a male hieratic élite, uncomprehending of life in the world, indifferent or opposed to secular value, ignorant of the feminine, hostile to humanist aspiration.

It is no answer to dismiss such apprehensions as irrational, mere bogeys from the standard repertoire of the enemy of religion. There is enough colour in them to call for notice. To the extent that they persist they will affect perception of the Church's *raison d'être.* And the daily papers furnish evidence of their persistence. A Church which wishes to be heard in the public realm must have a care for whatever may distort its voice.

There are, we saw earlier, different ways in which the voice may be expressed. Adapting an analysis made by J. Bryan Hehir it is possible to summarise these in a three-fold formula: prophecy, teaching, and contribution to the public debate.[12] As Hehir's commentary shows, these modes differ from each other in important ways; and different theologians and indeed the different Christian traditions have differing notions as to which is prior or most characteristic or most apt. It is not, I think, merely bland to say that each mode is needed, that they comple-ment each other, and that each has its own moment, to which the Church must be alive. All belong to education in the most basic sense:

each in its different way may help to evoke in the hearts of the hearers a recognition of the truth of the Word.

There is a sense in which the prophetic is the simplest mode—though not the easiest, for prophecy may cost life. It is simplest in being a direct challenge to response: the prophet's listeners are either with him or against. 'He said to me,' says Ezekiel of the voice in his vision, 'I am sending you to the Israelites, rebels who have rebelled against me. They and their forefathers have been in revolt against me to this very day, and this generation to which I am sending you is stubborn and obstinate. You are to say to them, "These are the words of the Lord God," and they will know that they have a prophet among them, whether they listen or whether in their rebelliousness they refuse to listen'.[13]

More complex are the other modes. The prophet challenges, the teacher must explain; the prophet speaks a burning word, the debater must persuade. The great simplicities of the prophet's vision sooner or later give way to the sophistication of advocacy in the forum. The other modes are neither greater nor less, but they are different. They are the modes which have been in question in the nature of this book, and it is their requirements which are now in question as we think of our critic and his—and her—unease.

Archbishop John Quinn of San Francisco has written: 'In a free pluralistic society . . . the Church has the right to make and to express moral judgments about public policy for two reasons: first, to guide and help in the formation of the conscience of believers; and, second, to contribute to the public policy debate by creating space for the moral dimension of these issues and by helping to set the correct terms for the public debate.'[14] It is plain that by Church Archbishop Quinn means hierarchy.

The secular basis for the right of which the Archbishop speaks is the right to religious freedom guaranteed now by civilised nations. Its basis in Catholic ecclesiology is in the mandate to teach which goes with ordination to preach and give witness to the gospel of Jesus Christ. But a juridically or theologically based claim of a right to teach will not by itself secure a hearing for what is taught. The two-fold objective formulated by Archbishop Quinn generates certain requirements of an apt teaching mode.

Some of the requirements scarcely need enumeration. It is obvious for instance that positions taken by hierarchy must be argued for, not just imposed. Distinctions between the core of the faith and its incidentals must be honoured. There must be recognition of the difference between principle and its application. There must be regard for lay competence and for the autonomy of secular affairs.

These ingredients of an apt mode are no more than is called for by the self-understanding of the Church articulated in the Second Vatican Council. But at the end of a quarter of a century in which the Church has sought to comport itself according to that understanding we should perhaps try to characterise more exactly what, granted the objective formulated above, an apt teaching mode now bespeaks of the bearers of *magisterium* in the Church. Its main requirements may be summarised as an acceptable style, a comprehensive integrated content, and an idiom which is intelligible to believer and unbeliever alike.

A Matter of Style

It may be objected at the outset that to speak of an acceptable style of authority is to take from the formal authority of the bearers of *magisterium* in the Church. They hold their office in virtue of their ordination and apostolic succession. Their authority to teach is therefore a matter of principle not of 'style'—based on Christ's mandate to teach all nations, not on weight of argument or reasonableness of tone. Why should attention to style be important or, indeed, why attention to style at all?

But from the fact that someone holds the post of teacher, by appointment or commission or even election, it does not follow that he or she will inevitably teach well. There is an art of teaching and there are teaching skills; and there are styles and modes of greater or less appropriateness depending upon the subject and upon the listeners. And even if the ultimate basis for a teacher's authority is formal—that he or she is the one appointed to teach—no one will in fact command a hearing if the laws of communication are ignored.

A style which is authoritarian will not work in the world of today. It does not work in politics for example, or in the world of industry or economics, or at least not in the long run. Still less is it effective in the leadership of voluntary bodies. There are Church leaders who 'lead' still by a crude use of power, but this has a chance only when the subjects of their ministrations are so wholly beholden as to be unable even to answer back.

But the essential objection to authoritarianism is not just that it no longer works: rather is it that this way of treating people is disrespectful. 'Contemporary man is becoming increasingly conscious of the dignity of the human person; more and more people are demanding that men should exercise fully their own judgment and a responsible freedom in their actions, and should not be subject to the pressure of coercion but be inspired by a sense of duty.'[15] The principle of freedom in religion is founded by the Council in the dignity of every person, in the light of which coercion in spiritual matters is especially inept.

But if authoritarianism as a stance for leadership is inept, what of 'paternalism'? This is an attitude which envisages people as needing to be protected, rather as one might want to protect a child. Protected from what? Protection is needed, so this view runs, from external dangers which threaten the welfare of the led, danger to which they will not even be alert unless the leaders watch on their account. But, sometimes more importantly, people need to be protected from themselves, for humankind is wayward and always prone to sin.

This is a reputable viewpoint which in varying versions has appeared regularly in the history of ethics and politics and the art of government. St Augustine, for example, believed that law exists *propter peccatum*— because there is in human beings a proclivity towards sin, in the curbing of which is required, among other things, coercion by the law. Even John Stuart Mill envisaged the necessity for paternalism in some circumstances; so, though more stringently, does Professor Hart.

But an attitude of protectiveness is at risk of deteriorating into disrespect. Christians believe that humans are made in the image of God and the Catholic tradition is that though sin flaws human being in the world it does not radically vitiate our potential for glory. In this light a view which sees us ultimately in terms of sinfulness is skewed, and policies of leadership based exclusively on such a view are not adequate to the Christian vision for humankind.

The vulnerable always need protection and a wise leader will have a special care for the specially vulnerable. But if this is not combined with regard for the gifts of nature and grace which in Christian belief belong to the new creation, growth will be stunted, maturing precluded. And so a style of direction which is excessively protective is inappropriate in the Church. If people are always treated as wayward children they may as well behave accordingly; though it is more likely that they will simply cease to heed the leaders who fail to give them their due.

An apt style for today will be aware of the nature of moral argument. Aristotle recognised that ethical reasoning does not exhibit the clarity of the mathematical,[16] and Aquinas noted that the closer to concrete circumstances a moral argument comes, the more difficult it is to formulate a clear and certain conclusion.[17] This need not mean that moral teaching must remain blandly general, and concrete options must at times be made. It does mean that no more is claimed for the option than is sustainable by evidence and argument; nor should a position be declared 'of the faith' if it is no more than one of a number of possible views, however strongly it may be held.

There is also the incomparable teaching power of witness: that is, the testimony of action and example. The Church speaks most eloquently to the world in its own involvement in the world's concerns. Presence to AIDS sufferers, the bringing of food where there is famine, active promotion of human rights—such is the material of credible exemplary teaching now. But this kind of witness is not just a pedagogical tactic; for these are not optional incidents of the Church's task but a constitutive part of its mission.

Another kind of active witness is imperative too. The kind of credibility which grounds an effective teaching will require also that the Church's own practice is not at variance with what is preached. When for example justice is called for by church leaders the call will ring hollow if justice is not seen to be done in the Church. A credible stance in regard to divorce will require those who take it to be seen to care for all the factors which make for a prospectful marriage. One who wants to persuade that abortion is wrong will not be heeded in the absence of a constructive care for women who may feel themselves driven to it.

Vision and Agenda

A standard criticism of Roman Catholic moral concern is that it tends to be restricted to the ethics of sexuality. The justice of the criticism must come in question when one considers, for example, the themes of the international synods held regularly since the Second Vatican Council, or the range of subjects canvassed in papal encyclicals over the same period. At the level of the local Church the two most significant 'teaching moments' in the US experience of Catholicism have been in connection with war and with the economy. In Ireland, while public controversy is still, it seems, most readily aroused upon issues of family and sexual morality, there are many encouraging signs of a widening of moral horizons.

Underlying these indications is a profound shift in theological understanding of the nature of the Church and of its mission in the world.[18] At its core is the espousal of what is usually called a social mission, the rationale of which is perhaps most tellingly characterised in the 1971 Synod's affirmation that the work of justice and participation in the transformation of the world is a constitutive dimension of the preaching of the gospel. A conclusive interpretation of this idea, it is fair to say, is still in process of discovery. But that it at least means that a social mission is at the heart of the Church's task is plain from innumerable magisterial statements, not least that from John Paul II which was quoted earlier in this chapter.

Yet there appears to be some difficulty for the Church in holding the social and the more interpersonal aspects of its ethic simultaneously in view and in an integral relationship. The difficulty manifests itself concretely in a tendency among church members to divide into supporters of either 'right to life' or 'quality of life' issues.[19] The former are primarily interested in issues such as abortion and euthanasia (and perhaps also capital punishment and war), the latter in matters of justice and peace. This is of course a generalisation but it is not without its truth; and the consequences have not been happy. For the divide has given rise to unproductive tensions in the Church, as well as weakening the Church's witness in the public forum.

It is against this background that there has emerged in Catholic contributions to US debates on public policy the concept of a 'consistent life ethic', advocacy of which is associated especially with the name of Cardinal Joseph Bernardin. The central insight is that there is a linkage between the several items of the Catholic ethic concerning life: first between those pertaining to the right to life, but also as between these and those whose reference is life's quality.

A general basis for the insight can be simply stated: 'Catholic social teaching is based on two truths about the human person: human life is both sacred and social. Because we esteem human life as sacred, we have a duty to protect and foster it at all stages of development, from conception to death, and in all circumstances. Because we acknowledge that human life is also social, we must develop the kind of societal environment that protects and fosters its development.'[20]

A more precise principle of linkage between the issues which concern the *right* to life is seen by Bernardin to be expressed in the rule that it is wrong directly to take innocent life. This is the principle which governs the Catholic position on abortion as on warfare, and it makes connections too with such problems as capital punishment and the care of the terminally ill. But though amenable to the application of this key principle these assaults on life cannot be collapsed into one problem; 'they are all distinct, enormously complicated, and deserving of individual treatment. No single answer and no simple response will solve them'.[21] For all that, they must be confronted as 'pieces of a larger pattern'.[22]

These issues are classified by the Cardinal as 'life-threatening', and they are distinguished from issues which are 'life-diminishing', among which he lists pornography, prostitution, sexism and racism.[23] But though distinct, this type is linked with issues of the right to life: 'If one contends, as we do, that the right of every fetus to be born should be protected by civil law and supported by civil consensus, then our moral, political and economic responsibilities do not stop at the moment of birth.'[24] There must therefore be a care too for the quality of life; indeed 'those who defend the right to life of the weakest among us must be equally visible in support of the quality of life of the powerless among us: the old and the young, the hungry and the homeless, the undocumented immigrant and the unemployed worker'.[25]

The moral concerns thus linked must, if the Church is serious about the social aspect of its mission, be brought to bear on public policy. In the US this has meant an attempt to contribute to debate on problems as diverse as abortion, nuclear strategy and capital punishment. But Bernardin is insistent on a 'political and psychological linkage among the life issues—from war to welfare concerns'.[26] And so concern for the quality of life, too, 'translates into specific political and economic positions on tax policy, employment generation, welfare policy, nutrition and feeding programs, and health care'.[27]

The inner linkage of the issues and the requirements of participating in public debate in their regard give rise to the need to create consensus. And this must start within the Catholic Church: 'We should begin with the honest recognition that the shaping of a consensus among Catholics on the spectrum of life issues is far from finished.'[28] I mentioned earlier the difficulty which church members appear to have in holding together the full range of moral concern which is indicated here. The difficulty was illustrated in reactions to the Bernardin proposals: in, for example, the complaint that attention to the ethics of nuclear strategy must lead to a watering down of opposition to abortion (and vice versa), and in a suspicion of linking of right to life and welfare issues. The Cardinal answered the critics by acknowledging relevant differences between the issues but continuing to insist upon the linkage.[29]

It was not intended to suggest that there was no place for special interest groups or programmes, or that each citizen must be actively engaged across the whole range of problems. 'A consistent ethic does not say everyone in the Church must do all things, but it does say that as individuals and groups pursue one issue, whether it is opposing abortion or capital punishment, the *way* we oppose one threat should be related to support for a systemic vision of life. It is not necessary or possible for each person to engage in each issue, but it is both possible and necessary for the Church as a whole to cultivate a conscious explicit connection among the several issues. And it is very necessary for preserving a systemic vision that individuals and groups who seek to witness to life at one point of the spectrum of life should not be seen as insensitive to or even opposed to other moral claims on the overall spectrum of life.'[30]

The consistent ethic of life concept as argued by Cardinal Bernardin is not free of difficulty at the level of theory any more than in its practice. Richard McCormick for example has pointed to problems which it encounters in terms of the debate on norms of which mention was made in an earlier chapter.[31] Yet it must be welcomed, as indeed McCormick also acknowledges, as a prospectful attempt to articulate a comprehensive and integrated moral vision for Catholic life today.

Such a project is important firstly for the Church itself: it cannot be right to make little of any of the issues comprised in the ethic's agenda, and when preference degenerates into factionalism ('I am for Justice', 'I am for Life') it is a scandal within the ecclesia. But it is a scandal also in the public realm, for it creates dissonance where what is needed above all is the calm voice of what John Courtney Murray called persuasion and pacific argument. A scandal is, literally, a stumbling-block; and such a stumbling-block impedes the Church's mission.

The Idiom of Persuasion

The point was made earlier that a teaching or educative role within the Church requires that ethical positions are argued for, not imposed. And if this holds in addressing the believer it holds *a fortiori* when a voice is sought in the affairs of the wider society. We have seen something of what this betokens as to Church leadership's stance and style. A related question is that of idiom.

By idiom here I mean a type or style of language, perhaps a kind of usage, characteristic of a speaker or appropriate to a subject matter. There is a religious idiom and an ethical, and ethics may be spoken of in the language of religion, as when we say that it is God's law that we should respect life or that Christ's will is that we should love one another. It is common among Christians to speak religiously of morals; and the mode has strengths and weaknesses, as we have seen.

But when Christians wish to speak with people who do not share their faith a religious idiom, it is obvious, will not do. Apart from its probable opacity for someone unfamiliar with the world from which it comes, the use of religious idiom in ethical discourse may give an impression that a moral position is grounded only in the tenets of the religion. This is regularly a problem in some matters of Catholic ethics—notably in the case of abortion, as is plain from recent public discussion in the United States.[32]

Cardinal Bernardin has made the point that an advantage of the consistent ethic of life concept is that it helps to 'build a bridge of common interest and common insight on a range of social and moral questions',[33] not only among members of the Church but within the wider society. But if that is so a common language must be forged: '. . . we face the challenge of stating our case, which is shaped in terms of our faith and our religious convictions, in non-religious terms which others of different faith convictions might find morally persuasive'.[34]

In the Catholic moral tradition the makings of that common language and idiom are available in the heritage of natural law thinking. In our time the concept of a morality derived from human nature and available to reasoned reflection has led to the concept of human rights. And this concept with its accompanying language is increasingly part of the moral currency of much of the world. It is an obvious basis for shared moral discourse and a common moral perspective, such as are required of contributions to public moral debate.

There is, of course, a prior question: are Catholic moral positions grounded in reason, or are there some whose basis is solely in the revelation from which the Christian tradition springs? This takes us back to the matters dealt with in chapter 3. A remark of Cardinal Bernardin's must serve as summary now—and what he says is applicable across the range of concrete ethical doctrine in the Catholic inheritance: 'The opposition to abortion, properly stated, is not a sectarian claim but a reflective, rational position which any person of good will may be invited to consider.'[35] Although Catholic moral teaching is rooted in and shaped by the Christian religious vision it can be accounted for in terms of rational argument.[36]

But this is the starting-point of a dialogue, not its conclusion. Each case has to be argued, and it is useless to pretend that there is prospect of an easy acceptance of the arguments in every case. Nor is adoption of the framework and language of human rights a magic formula. Many rights in the accepted enumerations are unspecific as to concrete content, leaving room for disagreement on what they may require or allow. A personal right to privacy is generally ackowledged: does it extend to giving a woman a right to choose abortion, as the US Supreme Court said? All codes affirm a right to life: does this include a right to life of the unborn? Are there 'Gay Rights'? What is the nature or scope of a right to food, shelter or clothing?

These examples indicate some of the deeply held differences to be met with in the polis today. In the course of this book I have thought it important to stress that there is nevertheless an encouraging measure of agreement, as between the Churches and among conscientious people generally. An undue pessimism on this score may engender in church people a siege mentality. And when this is coupled with a sense of moral superiority it precludes relating with even a minimum of grace to people of different persuasion.

The allusion to grace is deliberate. For central in all that the Church is or does is its call to be sign and agent of a divine grace. The heart of the Church's mission is to bear witness to the Word of a gracious God who loves creation and wills its freedom from the grip of sin. Its gospel is that this God is revealed in Jesus Christ, this deliverance begun in his work. Its mission is to share in the work of this salvation in all of its dimensions, including the transformation of the world. Its social mission includes a moral agenda. But the heart of the task of the Church remains the fostering of hope and the disclosure of grace.

APPENDIX

In their interventions in the debates concerning the sale of contraceptives and concerning abortion and divorce, the Irish Episcopal Conference have evolved a mode of address of these issues having three characteristic components. Adverting to a distinction between morality and law, they reiterated Catholic teaching on the moral issue; acknowledged the right and responsibility of the lawmaker and the citizen to decide what form legislation might take; and set out the Conference's own view of the measure in question.

A look at all of Conference's statements shows that the balance of the three components varied somewhat as between one topic and another, indeed as between one statement and another on the same topic. One way of putting this is to say that the bishops' opposition to a proposed measure is at times expressed more forcefully than at others. The reason for this variation is not evident on the face of the statements themselves. It can hardly be traced to 'growing conservatism', for its incidence is not chronologically linear. Nor is it relatable to the gravity of the issues: the first statement on abortion (1982) contains the clearest affirmation of the 'autonomy' of the political sphere, the second statement on contraception (1978) the least clear.

What are we to make of this? Perhaps the first thing to say is that the Conference's statements are not abstract accounts of the relationship between law and morality. They are rather, in each case, the concrete response of the bishops collectively, to a concrete pastoral situation as this is perceived by the Conference at the time. Whether or to what extent a particular perception is valid, whether a particular response is in the circumstances the most apt, is no doubt debatable—and debated, even among the bishops themselves. The point is that each is an exercise in the concrete application of principle, from which we should never expect the neatness of textbook treatment.

And so we need not be surprised if at one time there is a strong emphasis upon the question of the substantive morality of (say) abortion;

at another, more attention given the lawmaker's right to decide on forms of legislation; at yet another time much stress on what the bishops think will be the impact of certain kinds of law. The differing emphases reflect a Conference's perception of the actual requirements of its pastoral function at any particular time. But no doubt they also answer to certain underlying assumptions on the bishops' part about the nature and style of the leadership required of them.

So, for example, if a Conference's sense of its role is paternalistic its stance will be anxious and protective. It is likely to dwell upon the hazards which legislative developments appear to entail, and to be forceful in warning against them. It must, if it is not to be unfaithful to principle, concede the right of citizens and legislators to make up their minds as to what law is best. But the stress will be on its negative appraisal, and its recognition of the lawmaker's freedom will be more or less muted.

To some extent this kind of anxiety has characterised the Irish hierarchy's handling of all of the debates in question here. It appeared in an extreme form in the second statement concerning contraception (1978), which came close to discounting the principle that people are free to decide what form legislation should take. To be fair, this was not typical: an explicit ackowledgment of the rights of lawmakers and voters is normally made. One would have to say, though, that the dominant impression which the statements have left is of the bishops' resistance on the several issues in debate.

No doubt this is what was intended. After all, if the Conference is persuaded of the undesirability of a legislative development it is only to be expected that it will register its objections forcefully. And I am far from suggestimg that there is no place for a vigorous critique of measures which a community or its governors may have in mind. Moreover, the matters to which the Irish Conference drew attention are, by and large, matters which no serious person would want to overlook.

But that itself suggests a question. Is it always necessary to spell out considerations which no serious person would want to overlook? It may be, as some of the statements say or imply, that but for the bishops certain aspects would receive insufficient attention. Yet most of the considerations which their statements highlight are of a kind likely to surface in any public or parliamentary debate. Of course it may be replied that this is not the point: that what is important is that the bishops are seen to support or oppose this or that development, and the influence of 'the Church' brought to bear on the course of events. But this raises questions which are more fundamental still.

For it appears to suppose a view of the Church which sees it as composed of the leaders and the led, with the led being said by the leaders, in religious and civic matters alike. But this conception is untrue to the Catholic Church's self-understanding today. If it is in any degree true of an Irish understanding of the Church, what has to change is that understanding. It may seem to suppose also that only a church voice—and a Catholic one at that—may be relied on to do justice to a moral concern.

The mode of address in respect of questions of social morality which the Irish bishops have evolved has the makings of a methodology of constructive intervention in public debate. It is alive to relevant differences between the purviews of morality and law, and to the character of the bishops' competence in each of these. It continues to maintain the principle of freedom of conscience concerning matters which are not 'of the faith'.It displays awareness of the bishops' responsibility not only as regards the guidance of the members of their own Church but as potential contributors to debate in the public forum. But it may be wondered whether their long-term teaching and leadership interests are best served by the way in which these ingredients are characteristically handled.

For in the longer term it must be important, in terms of the bishops' own teaching objectives, that citizens and legislators are encouraged to assume responsibility for the shaping of Ireland's future. The moral and political maturity which this bespeaks will not be achieved in an ethos which is experienced as negative, anxious, untrusting. It will require 'education', in the precise sense of drawing out people's own potential for integrity and judgment.

And this must include an unambiguous recognition of people's right to make up their minds. If the bishops in a given case object to a contemplated measure it is their right and duty to express their objection as forcefully as seems to them necessary. But no less emphatic can be their endorsement of the freedom of voter or lawmaker to come without fear to a conscientious conclusion as to what in the end must be done.

Controversy in Ireland concerning the impingement of morality upon the law has in the main been confined to issues which bear, directly or indirectly, on sexual morality and what are nowadays called family values. The bishops' statements concerned contraception, abortion and divorce; but there has also been some discussion about the reform of legislation regarding homosexual practices, and the history of censorship of what the law considers obscene is famous. Minor if occasionally strident controversy attended the abolition of the concept of illegitimacy. There seems to be a kind of public touchiness about issues of family law generally.

It will doubtless be thought curious that the public repertoire of moral concern could be so restricted, and indeed the charge of a preoccupation with sexual morality is part of the standard criticism of the Irish Catholic Church. The charge is not without foundation, even if it is often made without apparent awareness that a concern with sexual morality is confined neither to Irish Catholicism nor to the Christian tradition.

But, for all that it may not be as publicly noticeable, there is evidence too of an expansion of moral horizons, and an increased sense of the claim of issues other than those mentioned above. Incidents and episodes as disparate as the conferring of an honorary degree on President Reagan and the blundering of Dublin County Council about the housing of travelling people at Mulhuddart have provoked indications, however modest, of a developing public sensibility as to the scope and character of the neighbour's needs.

Nor has the voice of the leadership of the Catholic Church been absent from these debates. Individual bishops have been to the fore in stimulating social action in aid of people who are 'marginalised', and a few have proffered a critique of public policy in their regard. The Conference produced a strong pastoral letter on justice in 1976; though one wishes that it had been brought to public attention with the vigour and persistence which has attended the promotion of some of the Conference's other pronouncements. The Conference's Commissions, especially those for Social Welfare, Justice and Peace, Emigrants, and Prisoners Overseas, continue to contribute to the sensitisation of the community upon a variety of moral issues, as well as engaging in valuable practical work in the areas of their concerns.

Other agencies of the Catholic Church which are contributing to developing public moral sensibility are the Conference of Major Religious Superiors and the Catholic Social Services Council of the archdiocese of Dublin. The former, especially through its so-called 'justice desk', has offered provocative analysis of current social problems; the latter has merited particular notice—and a certain quantity of wrath—for its animadversions on recent government budgets.[1]

These and like developments, evidence of an engagement of church leadership in the public arena, are by no means universally welcomed. There is a predictable irritation on the part of politicians and public officials who resent criticism from people who, as it seems, stand at a safe distance from the action. There is also the resistance of church members who think that the involvement of clergy and religious in this part of the public arena is a faddish (now somewhat dated) capitulation to the spirit of the age, a betrayal of the Church's 'spiritual mission'. And there are those who resent a church presence in the new debates for the same reason that they resented it in the old: as evidence only of an unquenchable lust for domination of the minds of the people.

But the Christian faith impels to engagement in the public arena; that has been so since the disciples of Jesus were emboldened by the Pentecost experience to bring their message to the market-place. Their message was in the first place about salvation, but from the beginning it was about right living too. And, like the mission of Jesus himself, it bore on what we would now call social issues: taxes, the law, the civil authority; the care of the widow, the orphan and the poor. Christian engagement with social issues can never be seen as merely modish, and if modern experience is forcing a special emphasis on this dimension of the Christian's call one can only be glad and grateful.

Nor does their faith permit church leaders to withdraw from the public forum. Their role as preachers of the gospel includes teaching the gospel's concrete meaning, and a moral *magisterium* is a part of this task; and part of *that* task is to contribute to public debate. But perhaps there is need to review the stance and style of the Irish Conference, as Ireland grows closer to Europe and the Church moves into the third millennium of its life.

J. Bryan Hehir has written of a 'public church', by which he means a church which is in conversation with the wider society. He says that 'its potential for shaping the public debate is tied to its capacity for moral persuasion—of its own community of faith and of the civil community'.[2] Persuasion in the community of faith now bespeaks a stance and a style which can meet the minds of a believer come of age. And in the civil community it requires an idiom which is intelligible to other traditions too.

Hehir says also that 'a public church should be activist, not by speaking to every issue, but by selecting those questions on which key political-moral choices are to be made in society.[3] This no doubt means that leaders will select questions which are actual in terms of the well-being of the people who inhabit this island now. But it involves attention also now to the fact that, bearing the marks of its complex history, our island people is moving into a new phase in the wider history of Europe. An Irish moral agenda will never again be domestic only.

NOTES

Chapter 1, pp. 6–15
1. Liam Ryan, 'The Church and Politics', *The Furrow*, vol.xxx, no. 1, p. 17.
2. John Whyte, *Church and State in Ireland* (Dublin 1976), p. 376.
3. Enda McDonagh, *The Making of Disciples* (Dublin 1982), p. 177.

Chapter 2, pp. 16–29
1. *Summa Theologiae*, 1a. 2ae. q.91, art. 2. The text and translation used here are those of the Blackfriars edition, vol. 28, ed. Thomas Gilby O.P. (hereinafter Bl 28), which contains Aquinas' so-called Tract on Law. The present reference is to p. 232.
2. Grace presupposes and enhances nature; faith is not at variance with reason.
3. Shorter OED (3rd edn).
4. *Tintern Abbey*
5. ibid.
6. cf. *Nicomachean Ethics*, Book 2. (E. tr. J.A.K. Thomson, Penguin 1966).
7. Penguin tr. E.F. Watling, p. 138.
8. Legal Positivism is a theory of law which holds, to speak roughly, that the binding-force of a law is derived by reference to strictly legal (as distinct from moral) criteria. Thus at Nürnberg, A.P. D'Entrèves notes 'the provisions for the . . . Tribunal were based, or purported to be based, on existing or "positive" international law'. *Natural Law* (London 1970), p. 106. Nevertheless, d'Entrèves believes, 'the boundaries of legal positivism were overstepped . . . the moment it was stated that the trials were "a question of justice"', ibid.
9. ibid.
10. *Summa Theologiae*, 1a. 2ae. q.92, art. 2, ad 4. Bl 28, p. 28.
11. *Law, Liberty and Morality* (OUP 1968), p. 1ff.

Chapter 3, pp. 30–49

1. *Dei Verbum*, par. 11. The translation used throughout this book is as in A. Flannery O.P. (ed.), *Vatican Council II, The Conciliar and Post-conciliar Documents*, vol. 1 (hereinafter Fl). Par. 11 of *Dei Verbum* is at p. 756.
2. par. 4, Fl 752.
3. Acts 2:24. The translation used in this work is that of the Revised Standard Version.
4. Mk. 16, and parallels.
5. Mk. 16:19.
6. Lk. 22:19. cf. 1Cor. 11:23–6.
7. Acts 2.
8. Is. 42.
9. Lk. 4:18, 19.
10. Acts 11:36–43.
11. Mt. 10:5ff.
12. Mt. 28:19, 20.
13. Jn. 20:21.
14. *Gospel and Law* (New York 1951), p. 13.
15. in Bauer (ed.), *Encyclopedia of Biblical Theology* (London 1976), art. 'Love'. (pp. 522–3).
16. See, for example, Isaiah 1.
17. cf. Bauer, op. cit., art. 'Conversion'.
18. in Bauer, op. cit., 'Kingdom of God', at p. 458.
19. in Bauer, ibid.
20. Mk. 1:15.
21. Mt. 22:23–40; Mk. 12:28–34; Lk. 10:25 ff.
22. Phil. 1:27.
23. e.g. Rom. 12, 13; 1 Cor. 5–8.
24. Jn. 20:31.
25. See for example, A. Robert and A. Tricot, *Guide to the Bible*, vol. 1 (Paris etc. 1963).
26. J.A. Fitzmyer, S.J., 'The Letter to the Romans', *The New Jerome Biblical Commentary*, ed. Brown, Fitzmyer and Murphy (Englewood Cliffs N.J. 1990), p. 830.
27. Rom. 11:33, 36.
28. Dodd, op. cit., p. 17.
29. Wayne Meeks, *The Moral World of the First Christians* (London 1987), p. 13.
30. T.S. Eliot, *Journey of the Magi*.

31. Meeks, op. cit., p. 13.
32. op. cit., p. 97.
33. Vincent McNamara, *Faith and Ethics* (Dublin 1985) p. 55ff.
34. op. cit.
35. 1 Cor 13.
36. 1 Cor 1:11.
37. Mt. 25:42, 43.
38. *The Moral Teaching of the New Testament*, tr. J. Holland-Smith (London 1965), p. 198.
39. Acts 11: 1–3.
40. Acts 11:18.
41. v. 1.
42. 15:6–11.
43. Gal 2:14.
44. Schnackenburg, op. cit., p. 200.
45. ibid.
46. 1 Cor 10:20.
47. 1 Cor 10:25.
48. v. 27.
49. vv. 28, 29.
50. Mk. 12:13–17.
51. D.J. Harrington, 'The Gospel according to Mark', *New Jerome Biblical Commentary*, p. 621.
52. v. 17.
53. Harrington loc. cit.
54. op. cit., p. 118.
55. op. cit., p. 235.
56. Art. 'Church and State', *A New Dictionary of Christian Ethics* (London 1987), p. 91.
57. 1 Thess. 4:10–12.
58. 1 Cor. 6.
59. Rom. 13:1–7.
60. cf. Schnackenburg, op. cit., p. 238.
61. ibid.
62. Fitzmyer, *New Jerome Biblical Commentary*, p. 864.
63. ibid. cf. Schnackenburg, op. cit., p. 241.
64. 1 Pet. 2:13–17.
65. Tit. 3:1–3.
66. 1 Tim. 2:1–3.
67. A.Y. Collins, 'The Apocalypse (Revelation)', *New Jerome Biblical*

Commentary, p. 998.
68. Philip Hughes, *A History of the Church*, vol 1 (London 1956), p. 157.
69. Schnackenburg, op. cit., p. 243.
70. Schnackenburg, op. cit., p. 244.
71. ibid.

Chapter 4, pp. 50–64
1. *Commentary on the Documents of Vatican II*, ed. H. Vorgrimler, vol. 1 (London 1967), p. 106 ff.
2. op. cit., p 109.
3. op. cit., p. 108.
4. *Gaudium et Spes*, par.1, Fl 903. (Hereinafter GS).
5. GS par. 2, Fl. p. 904.
6. Y. Congar, *Lay People in the Church* (London 1957), p. xxiv.
7. A footnote offers a quasi-apology for the word 'ecclesial': 'There is no such word in English: "ecclesiastical" does not quite express it, nor does "churchly" quite meet the case'. *O tempora, o mores* . . .
8. loc. cit.
9. *Apostolican actuositatem*, par. 2, Fl 768.
10. GS par. 43, Fl 944.
11. ibid.
12. GS 42, Fl 942.
13. Gs 43, Fl 944.
14. GS 36, Fl 935.
15. GS 16, Fl 916.
16. GS 28, Fl 928.
17. GS 40, Fl 939.
18. ibid.
19. ibid.
20. ibid.
21. ibid.
22. *Lumen Gentium* 48, Fl 407. (Hereinafter LG.)
23. cf. 1 Cor. 7:31.
24. LG 48, Fl 408.
25. A. Dulles, *Models of the Church* (Dublin, 1976).
26. Dulles, op. cit., p. 31.
27. op. cit., p. 45.
28. op. cit., p. 29.
29. op. cit., p. 187.

30. op. cit., p. 71.
31. Cited by Dulles at p. 72
32. 1 Thess. 2:2.
33. GS par 1, Fl 903.
34. GS 3, Fl 904.
35. GS 3, Fl 905.
36. Dulles, op. cit., p. 91.
37. op. cit., p. 83.
38. ibid.
39. op. cit., p. 86.
40. op. cit., p. 91.
41. cf. E. Schillebeecks, O.P., *Christ The Sacrament* (London, 1966).
42. Cited by Dulles, p. 58.
43. op. cit., p. 63.
44. ibid.
45. ibid.
46. Dulles, op. cit., p. 64.
47. J. Hamer, cited Dulles, p. 45.

Chapter 5, pp. 65–76
1. op. cit., p. 187.
2. cf. Dulles, p. 31.
3. Denzinger, *Enchiridion,* 966. (Hereinafter Denz.)
4. A good introduction to the theology of magisterium is in Francis A. Sullivan, S.J., *Magisterium, Teaching Authority in the Catholic Church* (Dublin 1983).
5. Denz. 966.
6. Denz. 960, 1821, 1828.
7. Denz. 1823.
8. Denz. 1839.
9. LG 25, Fl 379.
10. ibid.
11. LG 22, Fl 375.
12. This is of course the highest manifestation of collegiality.
13. LG 25, Fl 380.
14. Art. 'Infallibility', *New Dictionary of Theology*, ed. Komonchak, Collins and Lane (Dublin 1987), p. 518.
15. See John Mahoney, *The Making of Moral Theology* (Oxford, 1987), p. 116–74. Cf. Daniel Maguire, 'Morality and Magisterium' in *Readings in Moral Theology,* no. 3, ed. Curran and McCormick

(New York, Paulist Press, 1982), p. 34–66.

16. Cf. Sullivan, op. cit., p. 138 ff.; see especially n. 46 at p. 227. See also John Reed, 'Natural Law, Theology and the Church', *Theological Studies*, 26 (1965), p. 55 ff.

17. cf. V. Macnamara, *Faith and Ethics*, p. 12 (and references).

18. G.B. Guzzetti, 'The Church's Magisterium in the field of morality', *Readings in Moral Theology*, no. 3, p. 233.

19. *Dei Verbum*, par. 12, Fl 7578.

20. See for examples J. Fuchs, 'The Absoluteness of Moral Terms' in *Readings in Moral Theology*, no. 1 (New York 1979), pp. 94–137. This volume contains some of the main contributions to the discussion. A general introduction is R.M. Gula, S.S., *What Are They Saying About Moral Norms?*, (New York 1982)

21. cf. D. O'Callaghan, 'The Point of Intrinsic Evil,' *The Furrow*, 27 (1976), 7, pp. 406–11.

22. *S.Th.* 1a 2ae, 94, 4. Aquinas gives the examples of goods held in trust on their owner's behalf. As a rule they must be returned; 'yet a case can crop up when to return [them] would be injurious, and consequently unreasonable, as for instance were [they] to be required to attack one's country' (Bl 28, 89). Thomas adds: 'The more you descend into detail the more it appears how the general rule admits of exceptions, so that you have to hedge it with cautions and qualifications. The greater the number of additions accumulated the greater the number of ways in which the principle is seen to fall short, so that all by itself it cannot tell you whether it be right to return a deposit or not.'

23. A phrase used by e.g. R. McCormick and which he attributes to Donald Evans; cf *Ambiguity in Moral Choice*, p. 87 [1973 Marquette Lecture, reprinted in McCormick and Ramsay, eds., *Doing Evil to Achieve Good* (Chicago 1978), a key text for the debate]. See esp. Fuchs, art cit., pp. 125–6. This seems to be what D. O'Callaghan has in mind also; art. cit. n.21 supra.

24. LG 25, Fl 379.

25. LG 25, Fl 379.

26. Joseph A. Komonchak, 'Ordinary Papal Magisterium and Religious Assent' in *Readings in Moral Theology*, no. 3, ed. Curran and McCormick (New York 1982), pp. 67–90. Cf. also L Örsy, S.J., *The Church: Learning and Teaching* (Dublin 1987). A collection of articles and bishops' statements on dissent and related questions is in volume 6 of *Readings*. See also Sullivan, op. cit.

27. An Instruction of the Congregation of the Doctrine of the Faith which includes a treatment of this question was published in June 1990. Its text is in *Origins,* vol. 20 (1990), no. 8, p. 118–26. Commentary on this includes: F. Sullivan, S.J., 'The Theologian's Ecclesial Vocation and the 1990 CDF Instruction', *Theological Studies,* vol. 52 (1991), no. 1, pp. 51–68; A. Dulles, S.J., 'The Magisterium, Theology and Dissent', *Origins,* vol. 20 (1991), no. 42, p. 692–6; Archbishop John Quinn, 'Observations on Doctrinal Congregation's Instruction', *Origins,* vol. 20 (1990), no. 13, pp. 201–6.

This chapter was written before the Instruction was published. As regards matters of principle there seems to be no significant difference between my account of the nature and role of *magisterium* and the Instruction's. Two points however call for comment. (1) The Instruction states that 'It is a doctrine of faith that . . . moral norms can be infallibly taught by the magisterium' (par. 16). It cites as its authority Vatican I's *Dei Filius,* ch. 2 (Denz. 3005). This sentence in the Instruction follows an affirmation of the magisterium's competence in matters of the natural law and is immediately preceded by the statement that 'Revelation also contains moral teachings which per se could be known by natural reason', although 'access to them is made difficult by man's sinful condition'. Francis Sullivan considers (against Umberto Betti and Christian Duquoc) that 'The only naturally knowable moral norms which this document says can be infallibly taught are those which are also contained in the revelation' (art. cit. p. 57). Avery Dulles observes that the text from *Dei Filius* cited says nothing explicit about moral norms; 'it refers only to the fact that some revealed truths are also naturally knowable' (art. cit. p. 696, fn. 6).

It appears that the Instruction does nothing to clarify the questions left by Vatican I concerning infallibility in morals. My remarks on the problems of applying the notion to moral norms may therefore be left stand as a matter of interpretation. (2) The Instruction's account of dissent from authentic teaching seems tendentious. It may be, as Archbishop John Quinn has suggested, that the Instruction uses the word dissent in reference to 'public and organised manifestations of withheld assent' (art. cit. p. 203). He adds: 'If I have correctly understood the document . . . it calls theologians who under the described conditions feel they cannot give assent to a non-irreformable teaching to avoid using the media as an instrument of creating pressure and building up sides' (p.

204). If this is what the Instruction means one must of course concur. But rejection of this misuse of media does not touch the kind of question which is raised in my remarks.

Chapter 6, pp. 77–84

1. An account, including a summary of the state of the question together with the author's comments, is in A. Dulles, 'Bishops' Conference Documents: What Doctrinal Authority?', *Origins*, 14, no. 32, pp. 528–34.
2. *Economic Justice for All* (Washington 1986), ch. 1, par. 1.
3. op. cit., introductory section entitled 'A Pastoral Message', par. 20. *The Challenge of Peace* (Washington 1983): the text is in Philip J. Murnion (ed.) *Catholics and Nuclear War* (London 1983), pp. 247–338. See pp. 249–50.
4. Avery Dulles is one of the commentators who take this view: art. cit. n. 1, above. cf. also Dulles, 'The Gospel, The Church and Politics', Origins, vol. 16 (1987) pp. 637–46. Paul Ramsey and James Gustafson hold a similar position; cf. D. Hollenbach, *Justice, Peace and Human Rights* (New York 1988), pp. 185–6.
5. LG 43, Fl 944.
6. S.Th. 1a 2ae, 94, 4; cf. n. 22, ch. 5.
7. Murnion, op. cit., p. 249.
8. ibid.
9. Murnion, op. cit. p. 252.
10. Murnion, p. 249.
11. Texts are available at Catholic Press and Information Office, Dublin. A good example of the style is in the Pastoral *Love is For Life* (Dublin 1985), par. 185ff.
12. Statement on the law concerning the sale of contraceptives 1973.
13. Murnion p. 253.

Chapter 7, pp. 85–95

1. Mk. 1:15.
2. GS 36, Fl 935.
3. GS 43, Fl 945.
4. S.Th. 1a 2ae, 96, 2. What follows is in substance my 'Aquinas, Morality and Law', *Irish Theological Quarterly*, 1990:4 (vol. 56), reproduced by permission of the editors.
5. op. cit. 'De Lege', Bl 28, p. 3.
6. op. cit. 91, 3, Bl 28, p. 27.

7. Q. 90, Bl 28 pp. 5–17; cf also 95, 3 on Isidore's description of the positive qualities of law. Bl 28, pp. 109–111.

8. 91, 2, Bl 28, p. 123.

9. 95, 2, Bl 28, p. 105.

10. 95, 2 Bl 28, p. 107.

11. 95, 2, Bl 28, pp. 105, 107. Gilby translates 'determinatio quaedam' as 'constructional implementation', meaning to bring out the point that 'art adds something of its own to this process of making determinate'. He remarks that 'This is a key-passage in the history of state theory, and an early recognition by a social philosopher that pure legality and politics have their own proper interests which cannot be explicated in terms of individual and social morality.' cf. n. 6, p. 105.

12. 92, 1, Bl 28, p. 141.

13. 95, 1, Bl 28, p. 101.

14. 95, 3, Bl 28, p. 127.

15. ibid. cf. *Etymologies* ii, 10, and v, 21. PL 82, 131 and 203.

16. *S. Th.* loc. cit.

17. ad 2; Bl 28, p. 125.

18. Note however that Aquinas envisages legitimate differences in the concrete application of general principle (*S. Th.* 1a 2ae, 94, 4): see n. 22 in ch. 6 above.

19. 95, 3, Bl 28, p. 127.

20. 95, 2 Bl 28, p. 125.

21. Fl 799 ff.

22. par 1. Fl 799.

23. An account of the pre-conciliar position may be found in J. Newman, *Studies in Political Morality* (Dublin 1962), pp. 198–330.

24. loc. cit.

25. ibid.

26. ibid. Fl 799, 800.

27. ibid.

28. par 2, Fl 800.

29. ibid.

30. Fl 801.

31. ibid.

32. ibid.

33. ibid.

34. par 2, Fl 800.

35. par 7, Fl 805.

36. ibid.

37. ibid.

38. par 2, Fl 801.

39. Cf. Patrick Hannon, 'Catholics and Divorce' , The Furrow, 27 (1976), no. 8, p. 470ff.

40. par. 7, Fl 805.

41. *S. Th.* 1a. 2ae. 90, 2.

42. cf. Bl 28, Appendix 4, pp. 172–4.

43. par. 26, Fl 927.

44. J. Finnis, *Natural Law and Natural Rights* (Oxford 1980), p. 214.

45. A classic text is still J. Maritain, *The Person and the Common Good* (New York 1947); cf.also *The Rights of Man* (London 1944). Maritain's ideas on this theme were formulated against the background of the rise of nazism and fascism in Europe. An important modern review article is D. Hollenbach's 'The Common Good Revisited', *Theological Studies*, 50 (1989), pp. 70–94.

46. Finnis draws attention to a terminological problem: '. . . in much modern usage, including legal usage, "morality" signifies almost exclusively sexual morality and the requirements of decency, whereas in philosophical usage, sexual morality (including decency) is merely one small portion of the requirements of practical reasonableness. This ambiguity affects the use of the term "morality" even when it is conjoined with "public" as in the frequent references of the European Convention and the later UN Conventions (1966) to "public order or morals" And as for "public order", this phrase as used in the international documents suffers from the irremediable ambiguity that in common law systems it signifies absence of disorder (i.e. public peace, tranquillity and safety), whereas the expressions *ordre public* and *orden publico* used in the French and Spanish versions of these documents signify a civil law concept almost as wide as the concept of public policy in common law' (op. cit. p. 215). As Finnis notes, it is the civil law sense which is employed in the *Declaration on Religious Freedom.*

Chapter 8, pp. 96–109

1. op. cit., p. 214.

2. op. cit., pp. 216–18, at 216.

3. Cmnd. 247 (1957).

4. par. 13.

5. J.S. Mill, *On Liberty* (Penguin 1974).

6. Wolfenden, loc. cit.
7. par. 62.
8. Patrick Devlin, *The Enforcement of Morals* (Oxford 1965). (Hereinafter EM.)
9. EM 3.
10. EM 10.
11. EM 11.
12. ibid.
13. EM 13, 14.
14. EM 13, n.1.
15. EM 14.
16. EM 15.
17. ibid.
18. Lawyers' jargon for the man in the street.
19. EM 15.
20. ibid.
21. EM 16.
22. EM 17.
23. ibid.
24. EM 18.
25. EM 19.
26. ibid.
27. ibid.
28. ibid.
29. EM 20.
30. EM 22.
31. H.L.A. Hart, *Law, Liberty and Morality* (Oxford 1963). (Hereinafter LLM.)
32. LLM 16.
33. LLM 21.
34. ibid.
35. LLM 23.
36. LLM 30ff.
37. LLM 18.
38. LLM 30.
39. LLM 50, 51.
40. LLM 51.
41. ibid.
42. ibid.
43. ibid.

44. ibid.
45. Basil Mitchell, *Law, Morality and Religion in a Secular Society* (Oxford 1967), p. 18.
46. I.LM 4.
47. EM 15.
48. 'Mill on Liberty in Morals' in EM, pp. 102–22.
49. EM 102.
50. EM 22, 23.
51. LLM 17.
52. LLM 72.
53. EM 115.
54. ibid.
55. EM 100.
56. 'Democracy and Morality' in EM, pp. 86–101, at 90.
57. ibid.
58. ibid.
59. EM viii, ix.
60. EM 90.
61. H.L.A. Hart, *The Concept of Law* (Oxford 1961), p. 188. cf. p. 189ff.; and Mitchell, op. cit., p.23ff.
62. Devlin returns to some of these questions in the final chapter of *The Enforcement of Morals*, as does Professor Hart in the preface (the original English version of which I.have seen) to a Hebrew edition of *Law, Liberty and Morality*.

Chapter 9, pp. 110–24
 1. Simon Lee, *Law and Morals* (Oxford 1986), p. 30.
 2. op. cit., p. 34.
 3. J.C. Murray, S.J., *We Hold These Truths* (New York 1960), pp. 166–7.
 4. ibid.
 5. op. cit., p. 168.
 6. ibid.
 7. Richard P. McBrien, *Caesar's Coin* (New York 1987), pp. 165, 166.
 8. Murray, op. cit. p. 169.
 9. L. Örsy, 'The Common Good and Special Interest Groups in the Legislative Process', *The Catholics Lawyer*, 29 (1984), 2, pp. 146–50, at 149.
10. ibid.
11. art. cit. 149, 150.

12. cf. T. Fuechtmann (ed.), *Consistent Ethic of Life* (Kansas City 1988), p. 93.
13. But cf. Mary Ann Glendon, *Abortion and Divorce in Western Law* (Harvard 1987) for an instructive exploration of what she calls the 'rhetoric' of law.
14. op. cit. p. 232.
15. Murray, op. cit. p. 277.
16. See Murray, op. cit.; and *The Problem of Religious Freedom* (London-Dublin 1965).
17. 410 U.S. 113 (1973).
18. The lines of the debate are sketched in McBrien, op. cit. esp. ch. 5.
19. e.g. McBrien op. cit.; which see also for further references.
20. A standard account may be found in C.J. McFadden, *Medical Ethics* (London 1962). This reproduces the approach of the classic manuals; cf. D. Prümmer, *Manuale Theologiae Moralis*, Tomus I (Freiburg/ Breisgau 1953). Modern commentators include Richard McCormick, Charles Curran, Klaus Demmer, and Germain Grisez who—against McCormick and Curran in particular—considers that it does not justify the stance of Mario Cuomo and others in the present debate; cf.Grisez, 'A Critique of Two Theological Papers', *Homiletic and Pastoral Review*, July 1984, pp. 10–15, and 'Public Funding: a Reply to Richard A. McCormick', *Homiletic and Pastoral Review*, June 1985, pp. 32–51. References to McCormick and Curran's articles are given by Grisez. Klaus Demmer's account is in 'Der Ansprunch der Toleranz', *Gregorianum* 63 (1982), pp. 701–20.

Crucial to Grisez' critique is the proposition that support of public funding for abortion is 'a personal moral act whose object is direct abortion' ('A Critique . . .', at p. 11). This is a controversial claim; its basis is in Grisez' more general fundamental moral theology (see *The Way of the Lord Jesus*, vol. 1 (Chicago 1983), esp. p. 300ff.) I do not think that in either of the articles here cited Grisez has made good this claim.
21. cf. McCormick and Ramsay (eds) *Doing Evil to Achieve Good* (Chicago 1978), pp. 45–6.
22. e.g. Demmer, Curran, arts cit.

Chapter 10, pp. 125–39
1. An extensive bibliography on religion, morality and politics is reviewed by David Hollenbach in 'Notes on Moral Theology,

Theological Studies, 49 (1988), pp. 68–89. See also Hollenbach, 'The Common Good Revisited', *Theological Studies,* 50 (1989), pp. 70–94.

2. *Centesimus Annus,* ch.1. The text used here is as in *Catholic International,* 2 (1991), no. 12.
3. *Convenientes in Universo.* Tr. as in Flannery, (ed.), *Vatican Council, More Post-conciliar Documents.* (Dublin 1982) , at p.696.
4. Lk. 4:18,19.
5. D. Hollenbach, *Justice, Peace and Human Rights* (New York 1988), p.181.
6. ibid.
7. *Dignitatis humanae,* par.4, Fl 799.
8. This, broadly speaking, is the position of theologians such as W. Pannenberg, J.Moltmann and J-B. Metz: cf. Hollenbach, op. cit. pp.189, 190.
9. So, e.g., K. Rahner, E. Schillebeeckx, G. Gutierrez, J.Gustafson.
10. Hollenbach, op.cit. p.183.
11. *Dignitatis humanae,* par. 1, Fl 799.
12. J. Bryan Hehir, 'The Right and Competence of the Church', in John A. Coleman (ed.), *A Hundred Years of Catholic Social Thought* (New York 1991), pp.55-71, at 66-9.
13. Ezek.2:3-5.
14. *Origins,* 14:21, 324.
15. *Dignitatis humanae,* par.1. cf. n. 11 above.
16. *Ethica Nicomachea,* 1094b, 11f. Cf. *Ethics,* tr. J.A.K.Thompson (Baltimore, Maryland, 1955), pp.27-8.
17. *S.Th.* 1a 2ae, 94,4. Cf. ch.5 supra.
18. Important aspects of underlying theological developments are in Dermot A. Lane, *Foundations for a Social Theology* (Dublin 1984). Cf. Leslie Griffin, 'The Integration of Spiritual and Temporal: Contemporary Roman Catholic Church-State Theory', *Theological Studies,* 48 (1987), pp. 225–57.
19. T. Fuechtmann (ed.), *Consistent Ethic of Life* (Kansas City 1988), p.8. (Hereinafter CEL). This contains the text of 10 addresses in which Cardinal Bernardin developed the concept of the `consistent life ethic', together with the papers of a symposium upon the theme, and the cardinal's response to the symposium.
20. CEL 50.
21. CEL 19.
22. ibid.
23. CEL 30.

24. CEL 8.
25. CEL 8, 9; cf.52.
26. CEL 17.
27. CEL 9; cf.52, 70.
28. CEL 10.
29. CEL 16, 17, 19, 24, 29 and esp. 77–85.
30. CEL 15.
31. CEL 96-200.
32. Ms Ferraro spoke of her personal views on abortion as being a matter of her 'religious' belief; and later she was to speak of her duty as a public official to uphold the constitutional guarantee of freedom of religion, saying 'I cannot fulfill that duty if I seek to impose my own religion on other American citizens.' But she was not the only one to canvas the question in those terms, and indeed many contributors (including Archbishop O'Connor and Governor Cuomo) were content to characterise the issue thus. Inevitably then the debate proceeded on the basis that the controversy was at least in part about the scope of the First Amendment.
33. CEL 125.
34. CEL 10. See Robert Lovin, 'Religion and American Public Life: Three Relationships', in Lovin (ed.), *Religion and American Public Life* (New York 1986), pp. 7–28, 9.
35. CEL 23.
36. cf. Lovin, loc. cit. Richard McCormick, 'Theology in the Public Forum', *The Critical Calling* (Washington D.C. 1987), pp. 191–208.

Appendix, pp. 140–44

1. These remarks concern corporate or institutional Church involvement. There is, of course, a great deal of involvement by voluntary bodies under church auspices or religious inspiration.
2. *Origins*, 14 (1984), no. 3, p.41.
3. ibid.